WORK IS NOT A FOUR-LETTER WORD

IMPROVING THE QUALITY OF YOUR WORK LIFE

WORK IS NOT A FOUR-LETTER WORD
IMPROVING THE QUALITY OF YOUR WORK LIFE

Stephen Strasser, Ph.D.
Associate Professor
Division of Hospital and Health Services Administration
The Ohio State University

John Sena, Ph.D.
Professor
Department of English
The Ohio State University

BUSINESS ONE IRWIN
Homewood, IL 60430

This publication is designed to provide accurate and authoritative information in regard to the subject matter covered. It is sold with the understanding that neither the author nor the publisher is engaged in rendering legal, accounting, or other professional service. If legal advice or other expert assistance is required, the services of a competent professional person should be sought.

From a Declaration of Principles jointly adopted by a Committee of the American Bar Association and a Committee of Publishers.

Sponsoring editor: Jeffrey A. Krames
Project editor: Jane Lightell
Production manager: Carma W. Fazio
Jacket Designer: Renee Klyczek Nordstrom
Compositor: Impressions, A Division of Edwards Brothers, Inc.
Typeface: 11/14 Palatino
Printer: Arcata Graphics/Kingsport

Library of Congress Cataloging-in-Publication Data

Strasser, Stephen.
    Work is not a four-letter word : improving the quality of your work life / Stephen Strasser and John Sena.
        p.   cm.
    Includes index.
    ISBN 1-55623-398-1
    1. Quality of work life.   I. Sena, John F.   II. Title.
HD6955.S875   1991
306.3'6—dc20   91–25051

Printed in the United States of America
2 3 4 5 6 7 8 9 0 K 8 7 6 5 4 3 2

To Sylvia Dunn Sena

To Sarah Strasser

*Without whom work would be a
four-letter word*

Acknowledgments

A book is rarely the creation of its authors exclusively; it has many parents. Certainly, *Work Is Not a Four-Letter Word* would not have been possible without the assistance and encouragement of numerous people.

We wish to thank Sylvia Sena for her incisive ideas, critical comments, editorial suggestions, and moral support.

We also wish to thank Lee Bolzenius, the PSMS administrative assistant at The Ohio State University, and Melissa Kennedy, Director of PSMS, who did a magnificent job of keeping everything on the project running smoothly while we were completing this book during the winter of 1991. We appreciate the assistance of Sherry Thomas; her editorial comments and substantive suggestions were very helpful.

Special thanks to Paul and Claudia Dusseau and Jim and Judy Balyeat for their "little, nameless, unremembered acts of kindness and of love"; their timely laughter and friendship has meant a great deal.

We are grateful to Jeffrey Krames, our editor and friend, for putting up with us and for supporting our publishing efforts over the years. We also appreciate the sage advice of our agent, Jane Jordan Browne.

We wish to express our general indebtedness to our colleagues and staffs at The Ohio State University's Division of Hospital and Health Services Administration and the Department of English. Their support, encouragement, and patience will not be forgotten. We are especially grateful to Steve Loebs, chair of the Division of Hospital and Health Services Administration, and to R.J. Caswell, William O. Cleverley, Paul C. Nutt, Donald Newkirk, Sandra Tannenbaum, Sharon Schweikart, and Bonnie Kantor. The College of Medicine at The Ohio State University has been in our corner from the start. Special thanks to Manual Tzagournis, dean; Ron St. Pierre, associate dean; and Joan Patton, chief financial officer. We are also grateful for the continuing support of Michael Riley, dean of the College of Humanities, and Morris Beja, chair of the Department of English. These individuals have created a work environment that encourages professors to pursue a wide range of interests and projects.

Throughout *Work Is Not a Four-Letter Word* we share with you observations of and conversations with numerous individuals, critical incidents that were reported to us, and surveys that we conducted. To protect the anonymity and confidentiality of our sources, we have masked their identities. When necessary, we have altered their comments, without changing the meaning or intent of their words, to further protect their identities. To insure anonymity and to clarify our presentations, we have at times provided a composite picture of workplaces, people, events, comments, and relationships. Any similarities you may observe to actual people, events, and relationships are purely coincidental.

Some of the issues we have raised here and brief portions of this manuscript have appeared in Stephen Strasser, *Working It Out: Sanity and Success in the Workplace* (Prentice Hall, 1989), and Stephen Strasser and John Sena, *From Campus to Corporation and the Next Ten Years* (Career Press, 1990) and *Transitions: Successful Strategies from Mid-Career to Retirement* (Career Press, 1990).

John F. Sena and Stephen Strasser
Columbus, Ohio
June 26, 1991

Contents

Introduction

Work Is Not a Four-Letter Word is about managing negative feelings and emotions at work. It is about change and development and growth, about replacing the old and troublesome with the new and beneficial. Unmanaged, unregulated, or uncontrolled negative feelings and emotions will adversely affect your sense of well-being, your career, and **your** personal life. To do nothing is to relegate yourself to a working life of frustration, pain, and failure. To take up arms against these problems is to reawaken and restore the positive and optimistic feelings you had when work was fresh, new, exciting, and uncomplicated.

We have selected what we believe are some of the most common negative feelings and emotions that individuals experience at work, feelings and emotions that make literally thousands of people dread Monday mornings.

Work Is Not a Four-Letter Word begins with one of the most common problems we have observed in the workplace, the feeling that you are unappreciated and taken for granted, that your coworkers and especially your boss do not recognize or appreciate the contributions you are making. In the first two chapters, we discuss the nature and dynamics of appreciation, the multiple forms that it may take, a method for determining if your feelings are based on reality, and remedies for the problems so that you may receive the recognition that you deserve.

In our third chapter we take out of the closet one of the least discussed but most significant problems experienced in the workplace: boredom. While boredom can negatively impact the financial bottom lines of businesses—bored employees are likely to produce less, produce it worse, and produce it more slowly than their stimulated colleagues—the human costs are even greater. Boredom can be, as Mr. Roberts described it in the play bearing his name, "a terrible sort of suicide." We offer numerous practical and potentially effective suggestions for reenergizing your job and yourself.

Our fourth and fifth chapters deal with the problems of success: those who are miserable because they are *not* successful and those who are equally miserable because they *are* successful. For people who wish to be successful we offer 15 recommendations that have been gleaned from interviews with successful executives and managers, the professional literature of organizational management and behavior, and our collective experiences. As with all our recommendations throughout this book, we stress substance rather than style. Success to some brings not joy but distress; not elation but a hollow, empty feeling. In chapter five we examine some of the dominant problems brought on by success and discuss concrete steps that may be taken to resolve the negative feelings occasioned by these problems.

In chapter six, "Not All Prisons Have Bars," we examine the plight of workers who feel shy, vulnerable, or intimadated. If you believe that any of these feelings is preventing you from giving an appropriate representation of yourself, interfering with your advancement, or making life unpleasant at work, help is on the way.

"Popping the cork" does not always refer to opening a bottle of champagne. In chapter seven we discuss one of the most potentially destructive and disturbing emotions in the workplace: anger. We examine its major manifestations—the raging bull, the sly mouse, the bosom serpent, and the omnivorous shark—and, more importantly, how to slay these beasts.

The opportunity to socialize or to form relationships is one of the major experiences and benefits of work. This benefit, however, is fraught with problems: people who want to form friendships but cannot; friendships that turn into romances; sweet little nothings that curdle and turn sour. We take a close look at building relationships on the job in chapter eight, " 'I Ain't Got Nobody': Feeling Disconnected at Work."

We conclude with "Workhealth and Workplay," a brief chapter on how to introduce more creativity and play into your working life.

A BOOK FOR ALL SEASONS

We believe that *Work Is Not a Four-Letter Word* is several books in one.

It is a *guidebook* that will help you understand more fully the negative feelings and emotions that you are experiencing—why work has stopped being fun. Why, for instance, do you feel unappreciated, intimidated, angry, or bored? Is the source of the problem internal, external, or a combination of both? How do you go about resolving these problems? Do you have a realistic sense of the extent of the problem you are experiencing, or is it possible that you have magnified it out of proportion? Are you, for instance, genuinely being unappreciated, unrecognized, and unrewarded at work, or do you simply think that you are? Are you bored, or do you have unrealistic expectations of what work should be like? Are you shy and timid, or are you simply cautious? How do you determine the answers?

It is a *how-to* book that offers not simply theories but practical, concrete recommendations for how to manage the negative feelings and emotions that you are experiencing and how to work with or supervise people undergoing similar problems. We want to help you create a plan of action to replace the unpleasant, unpalatable, and unacceptable with workhealth and workplay.

We think that one of the primary strengths of *Work Is Not a Four-Letter Word* is that our recommendations are realistic, eminently doable, and potentially effective. For instance, our chapter on people who feel that they are on a treadmill at work, plodding away but getting nowhere, contains practical and specific recommendations for becoming successful or at least giving your career a boost. If success is not what you thought it would be, we offer numerous suggestions for getting the maximum benefits from your hard work. Throughout our book, we want to help you take control of your life at work and not simply to react to the behavior or conduct of others.

It is a *resource* book filled with information on a wide range of workplace problems. Some of them will be collaterally related to the primary problems that you are experiencing; some of them will be problems that you may encounter in the future if resolute action is not taken now. We wish to help you recognize potential problems, confront the black beasts that roam within you, develop your potential, build a successful career, and make workhealth and workplay a reality in your life.

Finally, *Work Is Not a Four-Letter Word* is a *personal* book. Everyone needs a confidant, a close adviser, a boon companion; we hope that our book will fill this need. It understands what you are experiencing and sympathizes with you; it is listening to your concerns and is responding with candor and, we hope, wisdom; it wishes to offer you confidence where you saw uncertainty, promise where you saw doubt, opportunity where you saw limitation.

WHO CAN BENEFIT?

Work Is Not a Four-Letter Word is intended for a broad audience. The negative feelings and emotions we discuss transcend hierarchical, economic, gender, age, and social boundaries. These problems effect the well-compensated executive and the under-compensated secretary or teacher; those who have stretch limos and those who have to stretch their paychecks; those who appear to have life by the tail and those who continuously have their tails between their legs; the shakers, fakers, and candlestick makers; those who are twentysomething to those who are sixtysomething.

Work Is Not a Four-Letter Word is also valuable for the family and friends of employees experiencing negative feelings and emotions. We are holistic creatures; our professional and personal lives are inextricably interrelated and intertwined. It is unrealistic to think that the problems experienced at work will not soon find ways of manifesting themselves to family and friends. We believe that we can help family and friends to understand what the beleaguered individual is undergoing, the causes and nature of the difficulties, and the reasons for his or her reactions, interactions, and counteractions. We think that our suggestions, advice, and recommendations will assist you in becoming actively and effectively supportive instead of feeling helpless, frustrated, and dysfunctionally codependent.

Chapter One

"I Don't Get No Respect"

Feeling Unappreciated at Work

J ack Roy tried his best to be a professional comic. The only problem was that his audiences rarely laughed. He soon left the roar of the greasepaint and the smell of the crowd to resume his earlier occupation as a salesman. Feeling unappreciated and frustrated in that profession, he decided at age 40 to give comedy one more try. Only this time, he talked to audiences about how he felt—his failure to be recognized or rewarded, his need to be valued, his lack of success. His comic refrain, "I don't get no respect," immediately caught on, and Jack Roy—or Rodney Dangerfield, as he is better known—became a hit with audiences across the nation.

He had struck in this simple line a sympathetic chord in people everywhere. Feeling unappreciated and taken for granted, thinking that no one recognizes your true worth and merit, imagining that your talents are going unacknowledged is, we believe, one of the most common negative emotions experienced in the workplace. It plays no favorites: it is experienced by CEOs as well as by their secretaries; blue-collar and white-collar, starched-collar and button-down-collar workers; young employees recently inducted into the ranks of the work force and mature, battle-scarred veterans; those who love their jobs, those who hate their jobs, and those who simply wish they had a job. Indeed, the success of Rodney Dangerfield's refrain and his act in general is attributable to the fact that he has found a common denominator, that so many people can relate to what he is saying.

While Rodney resurrected a comedy career by giving voice to feelings of being unappreciated, for most people these feelings are anything but a laughing matter. Feelings of being unrecognized, unrewarded, and unsung often raise emotional and psychological havoc within an individual. The sense of fulfillment and contentment that work should provide is replaced by anger, frustration, and withdrawal.

In this chapter we shall discuss the nature and dynamics of recognition and appreciation, the multiple forms that appreciation or rewards may take, and how to determine if you are being appreciated and recognized at work. If you conclude that you are, indeed, being ignored or taken for granted, there is no need to suffer in silence. We shall recommend concrete and practical measures that may be undertaken to remedy the problem.

THE NEED TO BE RECOGNIZED

There are numerous ways in which individuals in the workplace express their feelings of being unappreciated. The following hypothetical examples, not intended to be an exhaustive list, are typical of the complaints that we have most frequently encountered:

1. "Nobody cares about what I'm doing around here. I might as well be a piece of the furniture." (*lack of acknowledgment*)

2. "I bust my chops 10 hours a day, and no one even says thank you. " (*being taken for granted*)

3. "All I hear about are my mistakes or how I could do my job better. No one ever says a thing when I do something right!" (*lack of performance contingent rewards*)

4. "If I were to have a car accident with our divisional vice president, he wouldn't even know that we worked for the same company." (*laboring in obscurity*)

5. "I have worked in the dietary department of this hospital for 12 years, and not once has anyone from another department come up to me to thank me for a job well done. My boss may occasionally compliment me, but I get not a word from anyone else." (*lack of recognition from outside one's unit*)

6. "My coworkers don't appreciate all that I do for our unit. I help them look good, but they must think that if they gave me a compliment they would turn to stone." (*lack of recognition from a support system at work*)

7. "I work over 50 hours a week, and no one at home seems to think that my job matters. My family takes me for granted." (*lack of recognition from a support system outside of work*)

8. "I break my neck to support my boss, but he takes all the credit for it. It's as though I were made of cellophane." (*lack of visibility and stolen recognition*)

9. "You would think that even one of my patients would say thank you. All I hear about is how long I keep them waiting." (*lack of appreciation from the group one is serving*)

10. "Management thinks they are acknowledging excellent work by their employee-of-the-month program, but everyone knows that it doesn't mean a thing." (*poorly constructed reward system; pseudo-recognition*)

11. "I have been toiling at the same job for three years. My boss doesn't have the slightest idea of how talented I am and what I really could do." (*lack of awareness by a boss of one's talents*)

One common theme running throughout this symphony of discontent is lack of recognition. While the nuances and shading may be different, all of these workers are lamenting that the quality of their work, the importance of their contribution, or even their very existence in the workplace is not being recognized by the people who matter to them.

It would be unfortunate and unfair for bosses and coworkers to dismiss such remarks as mere grousing or self-indulgent whining, for these are in most cases heartfelt and sincere statements that go to the very core of why people work. The most obvious reason why people work is, of course, to earn money so that they can keep body and soul together and a roof over each. The less obvious, but no less meaningful, reasons they work are psychological in nature. As noted by Maslow and Levinson, as well as other organizational scientists, work and the recognition it can bring is a vehicle through which individuals fulfill numerous psychological needs.

THE NEED TO MATTER

Work is closely related to one's sense of identity. If you ask an individual who he or she is, it would not be unusual for that person to say, "I am a teacher," or "I am a nurse," or "I am an insurance salesman." While there is an obvious flaw in this logic, the fact remains that we generally ally *who* we are with *what we do*. Our work and our self-esteem, our work and our self-conception, are inextricably linked. We must know that our work matters, that others care about and respect what we do. If we believe that we are unappreciated, that our work is unacknowledged, and that our efforts are unsung, we experience a decline—in some cases even an absence—of positive feelings about ourselves. Instead of feeling worthwhile, we may feel without value; instead of feeling efficacious, we may feel impotent; instead of feeling good about ourselves, we may feel that our self-image has been tarnished.

Psychologists tell us that when an individual feels that his or her achievements are appreciated and believes that he or she matters to coworkers and superiors, that individual's motivation and morale at work will probably be high. When these expectations are not met, however, the employee is likely to experience a series of negative, self-defeating emotions. The individual may, for instance, feel anger toward his or her boss, colleagues, and the company. He or she is more likely to be hypercritical of management decisions, rude to coworkers, and negligent in serving clients.

The unappreciated person often feels a sense of frustration, that no one understands or cares about what he or she is going through. To compound matters, the individual may feel—with some basis in reality—locked in to his or her position at work. The sense of being trapped may arise from the difficulty in finding another job, the financial loss one would suffer from withdrawing from a firm's

retirement program, the loss of seniority in changing jobs, the unpleasant prospects of being a job candidate once again, or the problems of relocating an entire family. Regardless of the cause, the
result is generally the same: a profound sense of frustration, of
being caught in a nightmare without any escape route.

It is not uncommon for the individual who feels anger and frustration from being unappreciated at work to withdraw from his or
her colleagues as well as from various workplace activities. It seems
logical to the individual who feels victimized by forces that he or
she cannot control to retreat to a more manageable and predictable
internal realm. In time, the employee may even withdraw from
family and friends and thus deny to himself or herself vitally important support groups.

Ultimately, the individual may cease to believe that he or she
should be recognized, appreciated, and rewarded. The employee
may think, "You know, they're right. If no one believes that I should
be acknowledged or rewarded, it must be because I have never
done anything worthwhile enough to be acknowledged or rewarded. Everyone can't be wrong." At this point the individual
has hit the nadir in personal esteem and self-worth; the employee
has now ceased to believe in himself or herself.

Much of this sequence of negative emotions may be seen in the
case of Betty R., an administrative assistant in the human resources
office of a large eastern corporation. Betty was a well-educated and
talented administrator who thought that she was underemployed.
After watching her growth and accomplishments over a two-year
period, we agreed with her assessment. Her boss, who realized that
she was capable of performing much more than appeared on her
job description, gave her ever-increasing responsibilities. When he
was especially busy or absent from the office, he allowed her to
answer questions, give advice, and make executive decisions on
his behalf. Betty felt angry that her extended responsibilities were
not being rewarded. "I don't think that he appreciates all that I do
in this office. He allows me a large degree of autonomy, which
suits me just fine. I like being able to process a grievance complaint
from the initial contact with our office to its resolution, but he

doesn't give me the recognition that my peers in other offices receive. They receive flowers on secretary's day and complimentary notes when they have done a good job; I only receive greater responsibilities."

Each week she combed through the classified ads and *The Wall Street Journal National Business Employment Weekly* but was unable to find a position that would allow her the freedom and flexibility she had. Frustrated that she was doomed to work for an unappreciative boss, she became curt and brusque to both him and her coworkers. Rather than voicing her complaints, she preferred to remain uncommunicative. She eventually found a job in another company, but to this day she harbors resentment toward her former boss for failing to acknowledge her talents and her contributions to the office.

While we wish to use Betty R.'s experience as an example of how an employee may react to what he or she perceives as a lack of appreciation, this case also suggests several issues that we shall discuss shortly. There are, we shall see, multiple ways of rewarding and expressing appreciation to an effective employee. Betty's boss, who we also interviewed, believed that he was acknowledging and complimenting her work in an intrinsic fashion by giving her extended responsibilities and a high degree of personal control over events in the office. Betty, however, was looking for extrinsic signs of approval. If they had been aware of the different forms that appreciation and recognition may take, she may have been spared from the hurt, anger, frustration, and withdrawal she experienced, and he may have retained a valuable employee.

THE NEED FOR CONTROL AND EFFICACY

A second psychological benefit gleaned from work is that it allows us to fulfill our need for personal control and efficacy. Since so much of our lives involves events that are beyond our control, it becomes reassuring for us to learn that we can solve problems, deliver services, make decisions, offer sound advice to colleagues and clients, influence events, devise strategies, and complete projects. In brief, work allows us to feel personally effective, in charge, on top of matters, in control of events.

We need, however, objective validation of our perceptions that we have achieved mastery over our workplace environment; we often need someone to tell us or to show us that what we are doing is, indeed, correct, that we are making progress, that we have won the battle and carried the day. When no one makes us feel important or rewards our efforts or provides us with gestures of positive reinforcement—which may range from a letter of commendation to a gentle "thank you"—we may believe that our perceptions of control and efficacy are illusory.

This was very much the case for an individual who had been working as a quality control specialist for about two years: "I have always felt good about working here. I think that I am effective in my work, but I can't tell for sure. The boss never gives me any stroking, not even a smile. I have yet to be asked to lunch by her. I have this queasy feeling in the pit of my stomach that maybe I'm not as good as I think I am. How can I tell?" While suggesting the need for performance appraisals, his remarks also indicate the importance that employees attach to symbols or gestures of approval from their bosses. Without such stroking, feelings of control and efficacy may be replaced by self-doubt and uncertainty.

THE NEED TO BELONG

Work also satisfies our need to belong, to be a part of a group. Humans are gregarious animals; it is in our nature to herd together, to form relationships, to feel connected to others. Appreciation and recognition are important signs that we are accepted, even valued, as members of a group. A simple remark, such as, "Hey, Bart, you did a good job," lets the recipient know that others care about his work and regard him as a kindred spirit. When individuals achieve a sense of solidarity in the workplace, it is not surprising to learn that they are likely to enjoy their work, meet their workplace responsibilities with a high level of achievement, work well across organizational divisions, and display an esprit de corps to their units and loyalty to their firms.

Probably at no point in our history has American business made greater efforts to create a feeling of teamwork in the workplace, a sense that individuals should see themselves as parts of a group and not as isolated entities. Beyond common goals, values, and attitudes, the cement that holds an effective group together is the respect, appreciation, and recognition that individuals show for one another. A bouquet for a secretary who has worked overtime to complete a project and a luncheon to celebrate a hard-earned contract are symbols of appreciation that strengthen the bonds of group cohesion. A simple act may convey a strong and important message.

Work, then, fulfills a variety of significant psychological needs. When the pressure of conformity is high, work allows us to define ourselves and to feel that we matter as individuals; in a world in which we are often controlled by events, work allows us to exercise a degree of command over our environment; at times when we feel powerless, work permits us to feel efficacious; in a society that often alienates and separates, work allows us to connect to others. These needs, as we have seen, can only be fulfilled when people feel that their work is appreciated, their achievements are rewarded, and their talents are recognized.

AM I BEING APPRECIATED?

At first blush, this question may seem superfluous. "Of course I am not appreciated. Why else would I be reading this chapter?" We are fully sympathetic to your feelings of being taken for granted and unrecognized; we realize that those feelings are honest and sincere and strong. The answer, however, to the question "Am I appreciated?" is not always simple.

The very fact that you have a job, for instance, is an important and clearly visible—although often taken-for-granted—sign that you are valued by your employer. A commitment by an employer to pay for your talents, skills, and potential is a fundamental statement that you are appreciated. If your pay is greater than the remuneration given to people doing a similar type of work for other employers, the statement becomes even louder and sweeter. When you make monetary comparisons between yourself and others, be sure to factor in all of your fringe benefits—health insurance, paid vacation, worker's compensation, company car—which may constitute as much as 40 percent of your total compensation package. Since employees typically do not see them as expendable income, they often forget that these benefits are a part of their total reimbursement. One reason, of course, that we may ignore salary as a sign of approval and appreciation is that it is given with regularity over a long period of time and thus becomes a part of the workplace status quo, a baseline over and above which we wish to be recognized.

The question "Am I appreciated?" raises an additional question, "*Should* I be appreciated?" If your job performance is marginal, or if you are performing at a level of achievement lower than your colleagues within your unit, then it is unrealistic to expect compliments and reassurances about the quality of your work.

Answering the question "Should I be appreciated?" demands that you be brutally honest with yourself in appraising your contributions to an employer. Do you, for instance, consistently meet deadlines? Do you receive indications from superiors, coworkers, and colleagues that the quality of your work is high? Do you work harmoniously with others? Are you meeting the expectations of your boss and your firm? When we fail to measure up or when events go badly, we tend often to blame others for our self-made misfortunes. Doing so allows us to avoid blaming ourselves or admitting that we are not as competent, masterful, or infallible as we had thought—or hoped. When evaluating yourself, rationalizations must be consciously and carefully avoided.

In addition to self-appraisal, it is imperative to get frequent feedback on your job-related effectiveness from your boss. If your firm or unit does not provide formal evaluations of personnel at prescribed times, request a meeting with your boss to discuss your progress. Colleagues are also a valuable source of information. Ask them what they think of your work: Assure them that you are not simply fishing for a compliment, but that you would like an objective appraisal of your achievements. There is little point to living in a self-deluded world.

It is also possible that the answer to the question "Am I appreciated?" is a resounding "yes," but that you have misinterpreted or failed to hear the response. It is not unusual, we have found, for employees to ignore numerous signs of appreciation and recognition. When a boss says, "Thank you," when a client says, "You have been of great help to me," or when a coworker smiles and nods after you have made a telling point at a meeting, these words and gestures should be considered as expressions of appreciation and approval, as signs that someone has taken notice of and values what you have done. As one nurse told us, "It's the smile, the expression of relief and comfort on my patient's face, that keeps me coming back for eight more hours of work."

If you feel that you may not have been aware of these signs, you might consider starting an *Appreciation Log*. Record in this log the various instances when someone has shown appreciation for your work, along with the form in which that appreciation was expressed. An Appreciation Log for one week may look like Figure 1–1.

After assiduously recording the number of complimentary or supportive words and gestures that you have received during one week, you may conclude that the people you serve and those with whom you work are not blind or insensitive to the contributions you are making. We hope that by recording the form in which approbation or gratitude or recognition is given, you will broaden your sensibility to the variety of ways in which people express appreciation. We know of an employee, for instance, who complained bitterly that his boss never complimented him but instead spent time in numerous one-on-one meetings with him, talking about the work assigned to his unit. The employee remained disgruntled until a colleague pointed out that the boss only spent time with individuals whose work he valued. Failure to spend time with the worker would have been a clear signal of non-appreciation. The employee came to realize that the problem was one of perception: the boss's language of appreciation was different from his.

In determining if your work is appreciated, you may ask an additional follow-up question: "Are my expectations for appreciation too high?" When you complete a project, you are intimately

FIGURE 1–1
Appreciation Log

Date	Activity	Source of Appreciation	Appreciation Message	Form
10/1/92	Sales call	Client	Told me that I "lived up to my word" on delivery date of new product line. Message sent was that I was honest and efficient.	Verbal
10/1/92	Sales staff meeting	Coworker	Nodded and smiled approvingly when I told our boss that shipping delays are still a problem because of excessive paperwork, even though he considers our department the best in the company. Message sent was that he appreciated that I had courage to mention a problem and go on record as being critical of a process.	Gestures
10/3/92	Passing in hallway of office	Secretary	Stopped to thank me for getting sales reports in on time rather than last-minute rush. Message sent was that she appreciates my effort to make her job easier.	Verbal
10/4/92	Taking daughter to high school band practice	My oldest daughter	Thanked me for getting up early on Saturday mornings "after working so hard all week." Gave me my favorite candy bar for being her chauffeur. Message sent was appreciation for my work at home and the office.	Verbal and gift
10/6/92	Sales call	Client	Client I have had for one year told me she was increasing next year's order. The highest sign of appreciation to a person in sales is repeat business.	More business
10/7/92	Talking to boss on phone	Boss	When I told him my month's sales figures, he grumbled, "Not great, not bad." That's a compliment coming from him. Message is that I did a good job last month.	Verbal; negative appreciation

(continued)

FIGURE 1-1
Appreciation Log (*concluded*)

Date	Activity	Source of Appreciation	Appreciation Message	Form
10/7/92	Sales call	Client	I told new client that I could not lower my prices because it would be unfair to other clients. He smiled and shook my hand. Message that he was sending was that he respected me for treating my clients fairly—no special deals.	Gestures

aware of every ounce of energy, effort, sweat, and tears that went into its success. More important, you *feel* that you have worked hard. In contrast, your boss may at best have only an intellectual understanding of your work. He or she did not experience the personal trials and tribulations—the all-nighters, the working weekends, the sweaty palms, the endless worry—that went into your accomplishment. Naturally, you expect your boss to do cartwheels and offer you a lifetime contract, and you are disappointed at anything less. When forming expectations for your boss's reaction to your work, allow for the difference in perspectives between the two of you.

Paradoxically, some individuals crave appreciation and supportive gestures but are embarrassed when they receive them and thus dismiss their importance. A business consultant told us, "I prepare my public presentations well; I desperately want to be successful. Yet when I give a speech and the audience applauds at the end, I feel embarrassed. I am completely unable to look out at the audience while they are applauding. I can't make eye-contact with the appreciation. Then I forget the applause almost immediately and focus on how I could have improved the speech. Isn't that ridiculous?"

It is neither ridiculous nor singular; we have talked to numerous successful people who feel guilty over their successes and thus block out the signals of appreciation sent their way. One of the

most interesting examples of this phenomenon that we have encountered concerns a professional writer who felt compelled to buy
gifts for his friends with the royalties from his works. Doing so
allowed him to purge himself of the guilt of being successful and
making money.

This type of reaction is not unlike the feelings of charlatanry and
the impostor phenomenon that we shall discuss in our chapter on
the problems of success (Chapter Five). Guilt or embarrassment at
receiving praise or being successful is rooted often in a poor self-
image. The individual does not feel worthy of the praise or de-
serving of the recognition that he or she is receiving and thus
refuses to accept it. A bitter and circular irony occurs: the individual
craves recognition, assiduously endeavors to earn it, receives the
recognition, and rejects it because he or she feels unworthy, which
in turn causes the hapless sufferer to seek more recognition.

Finally, in answering the question "Am I appreciated?" we
should keep in mind the tendency to forget or minimize the positive
words and gestures directed our way. We remember criticisms more
poignantly than compliments, reproofs more clearly than rewards,
clients who frown rather than clients who beam, surliness rather
than support from a coworker, admonishment rather than approbation from a boss, the one fish that got away rather than the nine
we caught. Perhaps it is that speck of insecurity in each of us that
keeps getting into our eye and causing it to tear.

Feelings of being unappreciated, unrecognized, taken for
granted, or poorly rewarded are, as we have suggested, among the
most common and serious problems in the workplace. We certainly
do not wish to imply that these feelings are trivial or insignificant,
creations of one's imagination or reflections of one's paranoia. We
think, however, that a first step in grappling with these negative
emotions is to define their extent and our possible complicity in
their presence.

HOW DO YOU WISH TO BE APPRECIATED?

Socrates enunciated the first rule of education more than 2000 years
ago when he said, "Know thyself." Each of us is unique. Our perceptions of events, understanding of people, and sense of fairness

and justice are often idiosyncratic, rooted in the experiences that have made us precisely the way we are. An employee's conception of what constitutes appreciation, recognition, or reward may be radically different from a boss's view of the matter. It may well be that you are being told that you are a valuable employee but in a language that is unfamiliar to you.

To help you understand your preferences and predilections, we have constructed the following exercise, which attempts to discriminate among various types of appreciation, recognition, and rewards. Check "Agree," "Disagree, or "No preference" after each statement. Our objective is not to pigeonhole you—you may not have a clear preference among the alternatives we present—but to assist you in comprehending more fully the types of appreciation, recognition, and rewards you desire.

Your Appreciation Language

1. I regard a salary increase as the most meaningful sign of appreciation for my work. I would rather have this type of recognition than a sense of personal accomplishment or a good feeling that comes from doing my job well.

Agree_____   Disagree_____   No preference_____

This question raises a distinction between *external* and *internal* rewards. If you answered "agree," you probably prefer external expressions of appreciation and recognition. It is not difficult to understand why this type of acknowledgment or reward is preferred by so many people. As children we were continually given external recognition for our achievements and behaviors: a hug from parents for having a good report card, a gold star on a test that we passed, a trophy for winning a race, a bravery sticker for not shedding too many tears during a visit to the doctor. It is little wonder, then, why we feel so comfortable with external recognitions or rewards at work; they have a long and respected lineage.

External rewards are also easily identifiable. They are often specific and concrete, something that can be seen or heard or even touched. Their source is external to our work. The person who prefers this type of recognition or reward will likely look for expressions of appreciation from a boss or company in items such as a private office, a company car, tickets to the theater or a sporting event, bonuses, stock options, even a turkey at Christmas.

Internal rewards also have an early origin for us, but they are generally not as easily identifiable or quantifiable. Internal rewards originate from our work and flow from within us, from our sense of accomplishment or personal growth. Most of the teachers we interviewed, for instance, described the intrinsic rewards they experienced from watching the progress of their students. "My greatest thrill in the classroom," said Susie S., a high school teacher from Ohio, "is when I see apathetic students become excited over poetry. I can see an excitement in their eyes when they discover that they like something that they didn't think they would. I share their excitement and feel good that I have helped turn on a light. I am a teacher because I like being a teacher. I can't imagine doing anything else."

Mary D., a registered nurse from Philadelphia, described her personal hierarchy of appreciation. "Naturally, I am concerned about my salary; I can't pay my electric bill with good will, and I can't take gratitude to the supermarket. But my chief source of appreciation and payment comes from my patients. I am now caring for a patient who has been hospitalized for two weeks. Each night before I go off duty, she squeezes my hand and smiles at me. That's why I became a nurse."

We encountered similar stories of intrinsic appreciation and rewards: a trust officer in a bank who "felt good" when helping a widow provide for her future; a builder who described the elation he received in turning an empty space into a beautiful home. Although not as quantifiable as an increase in salary, one's personal feelings of worth and accomplishment and the appreciation, recognition, and rewards that flow from the people one serves are by no means less real or less significant.

Appreciation for motivation and talents may also be seen when a boss gives an employee a high degree of independence and freedom. Although Betty R., the administrator we described earlier, did not see the autonomy her boss gave her as a compliment, his allowing her to make decisions without consulting him and to become at times his surrogate was an explicit statement of the confidence and trust he had in her judgment, initiative, and effectiveness. The intrinsic rewards in jobs that give you a degree of autonomy are often great. Betty could experience, for instance, the excitement of beginning a project and seeing it through to its conclusion, the satisfaction of knowing that she was not simply another cog in the wheel, the professional growth that results from developing new skills, and the feeling of self-sufficiency and self-reliance that comes from making decisions on her own.

It is not our intention here, or anywhere in our discussion of the various forms that appreciation and rewards may take, to make value judgments. Certain types of recognition are not inherently superior or inferior to other types of recognition; they are simply different. We wish instead to draw distinctions that will help you define what types of appreciation you prefer and to sensitize you to the various forms that appreciation may take.

2. I prefer to have my work recognized by being given the opportunity to buy stock options or by having my firm pay for my insurance premiums or my membership fees for professional organizations. Other types of recognition, such as a letter of commendation, are not nearly as important to me.

Agree_____   Disagree_____   No preference_____

The distinction here is between two types of extrinsic rewards: monetary expressions of appreciation and nonmonetary expressions. There are numerous examples of the latter: a memo from the boss congratulating you on your outstanding work; a verbal compliment from a superior, subordinate, or peer; a smile or a thank you from your boss after you complete an assignment; being named employee-of-the-month; receiving a preferred parking space; use of the company's recreational facilities for your family; personal time off with pay; special assignments; written commendations or plaques for distinguished achievement.

Nonmonetary expressions of appreciation or gratitude, however, are sometimes ignored by an employee, especially if he or she is looking for monetary signs. If your boss prefers to give nonmonetary or symbolic gestures of appreciation and you prefer monetary expressions, the problem is not a lack of recognition or appreciation but a difference in the form in which recognition and appreciation are being demonstrated. By understanding your boss's preferences, you may conclude that you are not as unheralded as you first thought. Furthermore, your boss may combine both monetary and nonmonetary rewards. Since nonmonetary signs of appreciation are often overlooked during our hectic working lives, we recommend once again that you keep an Appreciation Log for one week.

3. I prefer recognition that is for me alone. If it is something that others are also given, I do not value it as much.

Agree＿＿＿＿＿＿ Disagree＿＿＿＿＿＿ No preference＿＿＿＿＿＿

This type of individual is probably highly competitive. He or she is likely not only to prefer singular recognition but also to regard this type of recognition as the only true sign that his or her work has been appreciated. Thus, this type of employee would probably not value an across-the-board salary increase given to his or her unit. Nor would stock options or a bonus given as a reward for group performance be especially impressive. To be meaningful to this individual, the recognition must be prestigious, personal, and unique to him or her. If such recognition or expression of appreciation does not exist in this individual's firm, he or she may wish to recommend its creation. Until then, however, we advise the individual who prefers singular recognition to value the recognition and rewards given to his or her group and to think in terms of being a team player as well as a star.

4. I prefer the carrot to the absence of a stick. I want my boss to express his or her appreciation by telling me that I am doing a good job. I do not want silence or an absence of criticism to be considered as a sign of his or her support.

Agree＿＿＿＿＿＿ Disagree＿＿＿＿＿＿ No preference＿＿＿＿＿＿

We suspect that most people would check the "Agree" response. Many bosses, thankfully, use positive reinforcement to express their appreciation and to encourage ongoing achievements. Not all bosses, however, agree with this workplace strategy or leadership style; some prefer to use negative reinforcement. Jim B., a computer technician, worked for such a man. "Everyday, like clockwork, he would come in and berate us for falling behind schedule. When he wasn't doing that he was yelling at us for having a messy floor or for leaving out our tools. It was always something. About once a week he would come in and not say a word. We knew that production was on schedule then."

Most people, understandably, do not react well to this negative strategy of praise-through-the-absence-of-blame. Jim B. was perceptive enough to understand the appreciation and recognition system his boss was using; he understood that silence was not only golden, it was a compliment.

We hope that our discussion of the various forms that appreciation, recognition, and rewards may take suggests the wisdom of the Socratic injunction to know yourself. It is vital that you understand the nature of your needs, the type of appreciation and recognition that you crave, and how those needs and cravings may be satisfied. At the risk of being presumptuous, let us add a corollary to the statement of Socrates: "Know also the appreciation and rewards system of your boss and your firm." Although they may employ a system of appreciation and rewards that does not conform to your wishes, try to understand and accept their expressions of appreciation and recognition as meaningful and sincere. By broadening and adapting your conception of how appreciation, recognition, and rewards may be communicated, you may find that your boss and your firm are not oblivious to your contributions. The form of the message is not nearly as important as its substance.

The foundation for understanding the importance of appreciation and recognition has been laid. We hope you now have a better understanding of why you and your coworkers need to feel appreciated and recognized and of the forms the language of appreciation may take. In the next chapter, we shall turn our attention to specific steps you can take to increase the appreciation, recognition, and rewards that most working people wish to receive.

Chapter Two

"I Intend to Get Respect"

What I Can Do to Increase the Appreciation, Recognition, and Rewards that I Receive

After carefully considering your own appreciation and recognition language and that of your boss, you may conclude that you are, indeed, not being adequately acknowledged at work. You may also conclude that informing people that you wish to be appreciated is a sensitive, even uncomfortable, task. Yet it must be done.

The conviction that you are being taken for granted or that you are unappreciated or inadequately rewarded is likely to adversely affect your work, your relationship with your boss and colleagues, and your own psychological and emotional well-being. Furthermore, the unresolved anger that you may feel may spill over into your private life, with family and friends its innocent victims as you scream at the kids, kick the dog, knock down two martinis, and take on the world. Doing nothing or suffering in silence will only insure that your feelings of anger, frustration, exploitation, and victimization will continue. It is better to light a candle, as the Bible reminds us, than to curse the darkness.

It is important to have a sense of how much appreciation you can realistically expect, for the ease and openness with which compliments are given and appreciation is shown differ widely among bosses and organizations. One employee we interviewed commented, "I work in a very professional environment. That also means I work in a setting where you are more likely to be criticized than complimented—much more likely. It's a fact of life, and I know this up front. So when I do a good job and nobody does cartwheels of appreciation, I don't get too upset. I know what the system can and cannot deliver." This individual's understanding of his work environment is laudable.

It is futile to go to a dry well for rejuvenation. Analyze what your boss and organization can deliver in terms of appreciation, and form your expectations with those constraints in mind.

HOW TO INCREASE APPRECIATION

We wish you to consider the following recommendations for increasing the appreciation and recognition shown to you. Some may be easier for you to try than others; some may be more appropriate for your specific situation than others; some may work for you, and some may not. Although there are no universal panaceas, each of these recommendations may be an effective antidote for overcoming or ameliorating the anger, frustration, or distress that you are experiencing. We are not suggesting that you fish for compliments; there is nothing more hollow than appreciation that is solicited. We do believe, however, that you have a right to what is yours, to what you have earned.

Discuss Your Feelings with Your Boss

We recommend that, if possible, you address the problem at its source. Ask your boss for a private meeting to discuss your work and your position in the firm. There are related issues to your feelings of being unappreciated that may be discussed at this meeting. You may ask your boss, for instance, to evaluate the quality of your work in general, the success of a specific project, or your ability to function as a member of a team. You may wish to ask for an explanation of the firm's promotion policy and for concrete advice on what you can do to enhance your chances of advancement. You may wish to describe job-related problems that you have experienced and your efforts to overcome them, as well as what you believe have been your major achievements.

It is in this context of counseling, evaluating, advising, and coaching that you may comfortably raise the issues of appreciation, recognition, and rewards. It may be especially helpful for your boss if you cite a specific instance when you felt that your work had not been adequately acknowledged, as well as the type of response or encouragement from him or her that you would have welcomed. There is nothing wrong with telling your boss that you enjoy a pat on the back, a verbal compliment, or a letter of commendation. When your boss does express appreciation, reinforce or shape this behavior by telling him or her that you value such feedback: "Thank you. It feels good to hear that you liked the report I did. I really appreciate your taking the time to let me know directly." A compliment often provides a comfortable context for remarks that will increase the likelihood of future recognition.

Honesty, openness, and politeness should be the hallmarks of this meeting. Do not assume an adversarial relationship; hostility and sarcasm are counterproductive. Nor is there any reason to hedge, feel embarrassed, or think that your personal feelings are too trivial to discuss. If those feelings are bothering you, they automatically become vitally important for you to discuss and resolve. Since one of the major tasks of managers is to maintain high morale among their staffs, your boss will want to know if you are unhappy or disappointed at work and what he or she can do to remedy the problem. This meeting between you and your boss, then, should be a mutual learning experience that benefits both of you.

We realize, of course, that there are some bosses who are simply unapproachable. If you believe that discussing the issue directly with your boss would jeopardize your position in the firm, we hope the following additional suggestions will help resolve your problem.

Rely on Your Coworkers as a Support Group

While it is satisfying to hear expressions of appreciation and gratitude from a boss, recognition from peers is also an important boost to a person's morale and well-being. Obviously, it would be embarrassing to ask for a compliment from a colleague. It is not embarrassing or difficult, however, to sensitize coworkers to the satisfaction and pleasure of receiving expressions of appreciation. One method is to be sure to compliment them on their workplace successes. A congratulatory handshake after they have finished a project or landed a large account, a smile when they have assuaged a recalcitrant client, a brief note of support when they have undertaken a significant project: these are small gestures that are rich in good will, graciousness, and kindness. By being supportive yourself, you will encourage your colleagues to extend acts of support and appreciation to you.

When a coworker does compliment or congratulate you, it is important not to trivialize what you have done or to affect mock humility. We observed one individual, for instance, who received a prestigious award from a national marketing association. When his peers congratulated him, he seemed to shrug off their compliments with nonchalance: "It wasn't anything, really. You know these awards are largely political; anyone could get one." Instead of politely saying, "Thank you," or "I appreciate your kind words," he made his colleagues feel foolish for recognizing his achievement and belittled that they have not received an award that "anyone could get."

Mock humility often offends well-wishers and succeeds in conveying not modesty but an overweening pride. Failure to accept gestures of appreciation and recognition with grace will dissuade coworkers from providing positive feedback to you in the future. Let them know that you are grateful for their support and that their acknowledgment of your work means a great deal to you. The good feeling that you receive from the compliment will then be reflected back to those giving it and should encourage them to continue their practice.

Use Clients as a Support Group

Clients are also a valuable source of recognition. When they thank you for your promptness or effectiveness or thoughtfulness, accept their compliments graciously. If you wish to reinforce this behavior, you may respond, "I appreciate your kind words. It is always good to hear feedback directly from my clients. You have made my day." Not only may your clients help you achieve professional success, but they may also provide you with personal fulfillment.

Make Yourself and Your Accomplishments Tastefully Visible

One way of achieving visibility is to wear a sandwich board announcing your latest success. That may be a tad blatant. However, if you wish your boss and coworkers to recognize your accomplishments and to express their appreciation for your efforts, you must first let them know what those accomplishments and efforts are.

Hiding your light under a bushel keeps others in the dark as well as yourself. If, for instance, after months of intense work you have landed a large account, drop a brief note to your boss informing him or her of your success. If you have suddenly thought of a way to increase productivity, share that idea with your boss while it is still hot from your brain. If your boss offered you advice that was instrumental in completing a project, share that piece of good news with him or her. If you have overcome obstacles in order to complete a difficult project, let your boss know with a brief remark such as, "Putting together a new marketing strategy that didn't imitate our competitors' was hard, but it is done and I think our client is pleased with the results." Numerous managers have lamented to us that they only hear from their subordinates when there is a problem and that they would appreciate getting some pleasant news occasionally.

Bosses like resourceful employees with positive attitudes. They like people who, when a difficult task needs to be done, will immediately declare, "Why not me?" instead of "Why me?" When you are given the opportunity to undertake a major project for your boss or to wine and dine an important client or to present a report in a public forum, grasp the opportunity for demonstrating your talent and commitment. Initiative is always visible.

Keep your coworkers apprised of your efforts as well. This will not only allow them to react to your successes, but it will also permit them to empathize with you when you have failed. Remarks such as, "I understand exactly how bad you feel," or "Keep on plugging," will let you know that colleagues care about you and your work, recognize your efforts, and empathize with your feelings. One way to insure this type of support, of course, is to always be willing to express similar support for them.

Use a Facilitator, If Necessary

Some individuals who feel they are unappreciated and unrewarded may be too self-conscious or intimidated to go directly to their bosses to discuss the problem. If several coworkers in your office or unit share your feelings but are unwilling to meet with the boss, you may wish to designate one member of your group to act as a facilitator and discuss your collective concerns with the boss. Since the facilitator is speaking not as an individual but on behalf of a group, he or she should not feel uncomfortable, embarrassed, or self-conscious in advising the boss that a problem exits and in offering recommendations for its resolution. Unless you are working for Simon Legree or someone with the sensitivity of a stone, your boss should welcome your unit's attempt to keep the lines of communication open and morale high. It is crucial, of course, to temper this approach with taste and dignity; your unit is not begging for a compliment, nor is it planning a palace revolt. Since some bosses may chafe at this approach, think through the positive and negative consequences of this solution before you act.

Look for Appreciation, Recognition, and Rewards Outside of the Workplace

If your efforts to overcome your feelings of being taken for granted, unappreciated, and unrewarded are ineffective, look for approval, recognition, and support outside of the workplace. Playing a sport, acting in a local amateur theater company, working in a political campaign, or coaching a son's or daughter's athletic team may supply you with the praise, acknowledgment, and positive responses that you deserve, desire, and need. One of the major benefits of work, as we commented earlier, is that it provides a sense of efficacy and esteem, the feeling that you are capable and productive and that you matter to others. All of us need to have these positive feelings about ourselves if we are to maintain our emotional and psychological health. If you cannot derive these feelings from your professional life, look to your personal life as an alternative or supplemental source of fulfillment.

Look Within Yourself

While public recognition of your work is extremely important, never forget that the ultimate source of appreciation is you. Look at your achievements (e.g., read your Appreciation Log), review the projects you have completed and the clients you have pleased, consider how much less productive your unit would have been without your contribution, and then take pride in yourself. How we feel about ourselves is infinitely more important than how others view us. If you received praise from a boss or a coworker that you did not think you deserved, the acclaim would not be very meaningful to you. Likewise, if a boss or coworker withholds praise that you believe you deserve, do not let it cause you to lose confidence in yourself or deter you from giving yourself a pat on the back. There is nothing wrong with recognizing and rewarding yourself.

We realize that it is easy, after having your work ignored by bosses and coworkers, to begin to question your abilities and value. When others withhold recognition, it is especially important that you continue to believe in yourself. It is also important to have realistic expectations about the frequency and intensity of recognition that others may provide.

HOW CAN A MANAGER SHOW APPRECIATION?

Since you may be a manager now or have employees working under you in the future, we wish to include a brief discussion of some of the steps a manager may take to be sure that he or she is offering sufficient encouragement.

In Aldous Huxley's *Brave New World*, when an individual was unhappy or depressed, he or she had only to take a dose of a drug called "soma" in order to feel better. Although managers do not have access to Huxley's fictional drug, they are able to administer potions of appreciation, recognition, approval, praise, and rewards to their subordinates. These elixirs are powerful morale boosters and excellent reinforcers of the behaviors that managers desire in the workplace.

Your greatest strength as a manager lies in the effectiveness of your subordinates; when they perform well, you perform well and look good. Conveying your appreciation for their contributions is a vital element in maximizing their talents and tenacity. Your gestures of appreciation and recognition may contribute to increased productivity, improved quality of work, high morale, a decline in absenteeism and turnover, and increased loyalty to you and the firm. To assist you in demonstrating to your employees that you care about them and their welfare, and that you appreciate their contributions to your unit, we wish to make the following recommendations.

Hold Frequent Evaluation and Job-Counseling Sessions

Even if your firm has a formal policy of employee evaluation, letting a subordinate know how well he or she is performing is too important to occur only once or twice a year. Work review sessions are an excellent time to compliment an employee and to let the individual know how much you and the firm value his or her work. Since approval is probably most meaningful if it is given right after it has been earned, we advise holding a meeting immediately after the employee has completed a major project or any work worth recognizing.

You do not, of course, have to arrange a meeting with an employee every time you wish to compliment him or her. Allow spontaneous expressions of appreciation to flow naturally and honestly. Rarely will so much good will be gained by such little effort.

Some managers are uncomfortable, even embarrassed, at showing appreciation. If you fall into this category, designate a pinch hitter—another manager or a subordinate—to express your gratitude to a worker or a unit.

Consolation and solace are also a type of appreciation. If an employee has not been able to complete a project successfully, or if he or she is having difficulty at work, sympathy and encouragement will let the individual know that you are supportive and care about his or her welfare.

Be Creative in Demonstrating Appreciation and Recognition

Demonstrating appreciation through salary raises, bonuses, and other monetary awards is important, but the financial or resource constraints of your department or firm may preclude widespread use of these methods. Furthermore, research has indicated that under certain circumstances, extrinsic reward programs can undermine intrinsic motivation.[1]

Offering the same types of appreciation, recognition, and rewards year after year may have a tendency to reduce their positive impact. Instead of being tied to the time-worn practices of the past, create a variety of methods to show appreciation: an employee recognition program, extra vacation time, special assignments, flexible work schedules, letters of commendation, lunch with the boss, a luncheon or dinner sponsored by the firm in honor of an employee, time off from work, tuition payment for academic or professional courses, a paid trip to a professional meeting, a larger office, a redecorated office or an improved work area, tickets to a sporting event or the theater, a reserved parking space—these are all rewards. Employees who respond particularly well to intrinsic rewards may feel more appreciated if you ask them to serve as mentors for less experienced employees, give them greater responsibilities, or allow them more independence in completing their work. You may even wish to try a cafeteria approach, in which the employee may select from a variety of rewards the one that he or she values most.

---

1. E.L. Deci, *Intrinsic Motivation: Research and Theory* (New York: Plenum, 1975).

Learn the Employee's Language of Appreciation and Try to Speak It

The most effective forms of appreciation, recognition, and reward are forms that the employee values. Ask your subordinates how they would like to be recognized and rewarded, and adopt those suggestions whenever possible. If you find that their vision is narrow, you may try to sensitize them to the many ways that a boss may express his or her appreciation. It is important for you and your subordinates to speak the same language or to learn each other's.

Jim B., the head of an environmental office, told us that he always gave the most difficult assignments to the employees he regarded as the most talented or reliable. "One day my best person complained that I was picking on her by giving her problems to solve that no one else wanted to touch. I explained that tough assignments were my way of recognizing her abilities and complimenting her past work. She looked pleased and said, 'Thank you, I think.' "

Follow the Golden Rule

Place yourself in your employee's shoes. How would you feel if you made your employee's contribution and received the same degree of appreciation, recognition, and rewards that have been extended to him or her? Try to make the gestures of approval fit the importance and quality of the employee's contribution.

If an employee follows our earlier suggestion and asks to meet with you to discuss what he or she perceives as a lack of appreciation, react with the sensitivity and fairness that you would desire from your boss.

Be a Good Listener

Being elevated to a managerial position does not automatically confer omniscience. Your employees, individually and collectively, can teach you an enormous amount about your unit. Listen attentively to what they say. Whenever possible, get out of your office and meet them on their turf. Doing so will send them the message that you want to understand their problems from their perspectives, that you want to stay connected to them. If they say they feel neglected or overlooked by you, do not underestimate the depth and intensity of their feelings. If you can resolve an issue, tell them what you intend to do. If it is not within your power to grant their wishes, explain the constraints under which you work.

Do Not Steal Appreciation that Belongs to Your Employees

If the overall performance of your unit is praised, be sure to reflect that praise back to your employees. If they have worked hard and have helped you look good, tell other individuals in the organization about their contributions. And let your employees know that you have openly and publicly complimented them.

Do Not Forget about Intrinsic Rewards

Unlike extrinsic rewards, such as salary raises and promotions, intrinsic rewards derive from the job itself: they are the good feeling, sense of accomplishment, enjoyment, and satisfaction that one receives in performing a specific task. Research shows that care must be taken in administering extrinsic rewards, for if they are not directly tied to good performance or if they are perceived as being manipulative, they can undermine the intrinsic motivation of an employee.

Generally, intrinsic rewards can be powerful. One of the important—but least recognized—responsibilities of a manager is to help employees recognize the intrinsic benefits of their work.

Little Things Mean a Lot

There are numerous other gestures of appreciation which will be welcomed by your subordinates:

Brief Verbal Reinforcement.   Do not spare words such as "thank you," "well done," "good job," "great idea."

Nonverbal Support.   A smile, a nod of approval, or a handshake, may speak volumes to a subordinate.

An Apology.   If you have made a mistake, misunderstood a subordinate, or misspoken, do not hesitate to apologize.

Time.   Time is a precious commodity for everyone, not simply managers. If a subordinate has performed well, granting him or her time off, permission to arrive late for work, flexible time, personal time, or time to relax will be a significant sign of appreciation.

Treating Subordinates as Adults.   No one likes to be patronized. Subordinates must be treated as intelligent adults who have a vested interest in the success of their work and the productivity of their unit. Listening to your employees' concerns, involving them in the decision-making process when appropriate, and treating them with respect and courtesy will go far in maintaining high morale.

Honesty.   Telling subordinates you will take their concerns to top management and then failing to do so, making promises you cannot keep (even though your intentions may be benign), false posturing, or being misleading about future rewards will destroy your credibility and the morale of your unit. Do not hesitate to give negative feedback when it is deserved; if subordinates know that you are honest and your words are sincere, a compliment will carry great weight.

You.   Your personal presence will often convey your appreciation of your employees' work and your concern over their welfare. Talking to subordinates at their work stations, visiting the graveyard shift, and maintaining an open-door policy as much as possible will let people know that you appreciate them and value their contributions.

Appreciation and recognition of employees and their accomplishments are vital for maintaining an emotionally healthy and productive workplace. While feelings of being unappreciated, unrecognized, and taken for granted are widespread, we have found that some employees are reluctant or embarrassed to talk about these negative feelings to their coworkers or bosses. We hope that our discussion has taken these feelings out of the closet and exposed them to the light of day, where they may be analyzed, understood, and resolved.

To suppress feelings of being unappreciated, unrecognized, and unrewarded will only allow wounds to fester and adversely affect the quality of your work, as well as your emotional and psychological health. While the feeling of being unappreciated is painful, you hold the antidote in your hands. Ultimately, you and you alone are responsible for getting the appreciation you deserve. The good news is that it is not that difficult to do.

Chapter Three

Watching the Grass Grow

Boredom in the Workplace

Against boredom, even the Gods despair.

—Nietzsche

I've discovered, Doc, that the unseen enemy of this war is the boredom that eventually becomes a faith and, therefore, a terrible sort of suicide— and I know now that the ones who refuse to surrender to it are the strongest of all.

—Mr. Roberts

P erhaps you have observed or lived through one or more of the following hypothetical scenarios.

Scenario 1: Playing with Only Two Notes. Mary W., R.N., had spent $60,000 and four years of her life to earn a baccalaureate degree in nursing. She loved the idea of combining high tech with soft touch to help patients get well. She was taught in school that she was a fundamental part of the medical care team and that she would be able to make maximum use of her skills and knowledge in the nursing profession.

After working for a brief period of time, however, she became disillusioned, frustrated, and even a little angry. "I'm using about five percent of what I learned in nursing school. I'm not a part of anyone's medical care team. When I talk to physicians, they never listen to me; they treat me like a servant. I don't know why I bothered to go to school. I feel like a musician who is only allowed to play two notes."

Scenario 2: Words, Words, Words.   "It is absolutely remarkable," said one of Ralph B.'s coworkers, "how much of his day he spends chatting. First he's on the phone with family and friends. Then someone comes by his office, and he talks for another hour about office politics. Then it's time for lunch, where he holds court. Ralph is bright and creative, but he does very little at work. I can only explain him in one of three ways: he's lazy, he's bored, or he's both."

Scenario 3: Oh, My Aching Back.   Jim B. had recently been fired for the second time for absenteeism. "I am not lazy," he assured us, "nor am I a hypochondriac." It was as though life itself had conspired against him. Occasionally his alarm did not go off, and he missed the first few hours of work. Sometimes he missed his bus; he had gotten up on time, but he simply managed to miss it. "I also stay at home when I feel aches and pains in my shoulders and back. I went once to our company physician, but he couldn't find a physical basis for my complaints."

Scenario 4: Yawning to Death.   "If there is one thing that I hate about my job," remarked RoseAnn M., a composition teacher at a large metropolitan community college, "it's grading papers. I challenge anyone to read over 100 essays a week without yawning herself to death."

The individuals in these four scenarios all suffer from the same workplace malady: boredom. While it may be most easily seen in the last scenario, boredom is responsible for the feelings, attitudes, and behaviors exhibited in the other scenarios as well.

Boredom is, we believe, one of the least discussed but most powerful problems experienced in the workplace. We wish in this chapter to help you identify the sources of your boredom and to whisk it away from you and your job.

THE WORKPLACE COSTS OF BOREDOM

We read frequently about the financial costs of smoking or substance abuse in the workplace, but we rarely read or hear about the costs of boredom.

Cost 1: "I Don't Care Anymore."   Boredom often leads to indifference or apathy, which, in turn, negatively impacts productivity. The indifferent or apathetic employee is likely to produce less, produce it worse, and produce it more slowly than the stimulated or interested individual. The bored individual will often lose pride in the quality of his or her work and in the job itself.

At times, boredom can have even greater consequences. A pilot we interviewed told us that he is afraid of three things while he is flying: "weather, air traffic, and *boredom.*" Boredom, he discovered, impeded his ability to concentrate, to attend to the task at hand, and to keep a sharp edge.

Cost 2: Psychological Withdrawal from Work.   It should not be surprising that boredom is, as in the case of Jim B., a fundamental cause of absenteeism, tardiness, and employee turnover. A bored individual will not be stimulated to go to work, to arrive on time, to maintain motivation in a job, or to remain loyal to a company.

Cost 3: Procrastination.   If one of the truisms about human nature is that people seek pleasure and avoid pain, then it should not be surprising that boredom leads directly to putting off certain tasks, missing deadlines, postponing decisions, failing to complete assignments. The workplace abounds with euphemisms—"we put it on the back burner," "we put it on hold for a while," "the job just fell between the cracks"—for the procrastination spawned by boredom.

THE HUMAN COSTS OF BOREDOM

Cost 1: Negative Emotions and Behaviors. When expectations for interesting and challenging work are high and the job proves to be routine, the individual may experience, as in the case of nurse Mary W., disillusionment, frustration, and even anger. Individuals who are bored at their work because they think they are under-employed, or that their skills and talents are not being adequately used, frequently harbor resentment, disenchantment, or irritation toward their employers. We have often seen this occur with college students who have spent literally thousands of hours preparing themselves for stimulating and challenging work but who find themselves employed at relatively undemanding, repetitive tasks.

Cost 2: Stress. When we think of stress we are likely to conjure up images of frenzied traders on the floor of the New York Stock Exchange; overburdened emergency-room nurses and physicians desperately trying to save a life; or worried managers, complete with sweaty palms, trying to meet deadlines set by their biggest clients.

While job overload, complex activities, and grave responsibilities are classic causes of stress, so, too, is boredom. It is stressful to spend an eight-hour day in an unstimulating environment; it is stressful not to be able to use the skills and abilities you have worked so long and hard to develop; it is stressful not to have the opportunity to work on challenging problems; it is stressful not to be able to accomplish the goals you set for yourself; it is stressful to realize that you are not growing or developing or reaching your potential.

Cost 3: Death-in-Life. In a metaphoric sense, boredom is, as Mr. Roberts describes it, "a terrible sort of suicide." Boredom robs us of our passion: it does not allow us to feel the excitement of a new challenge, the satisfaction of working with colleagues, the sadness of failing, the joy of completing a difficult project. It undermines the pride we have in ourselves and the good feelings we experience from being productive. Boredom worships at the altars of routine and conformity and eschews the imaginative, the new, the inventive, and the romantic. Boredom—not crime or disease or drugs—may be the greatest threat to life that we confront. It destroys our motivation, energy, creativity, and spontaneity and leaves in its wake spiritless, listless individuals whose minds are on hold—workplace zombies.

SOLUTIONS TO BOREDOM ON THE JOB

"Wake Up! You're Bored." Self-Learning about Boredom

Realize that You Are Suffering from Boredom. Unlike many negative feelings, boredom can creep into your work life so insidiously and subtly that you may not realize fully that you are bored. Some individuals we talked to, for instance, described the dearth of stimulation and interest they felt at work but did not think that this was unusual. A high degree of boredom had become so much a part of their working lives that they assumed it was intrinsic to the workplace, that it simply went with the territory.

Boredom may also be hard to recognize because like Hydra, the multi-headed sea monster of classical mythology, it may have many manifestations: indifference, anger, disillusionment, procrastination, gossiping, physical aches and pains, headaches, avoidance of work, tardiness, absenteeism. You cannot overcome a problem unless you first realize that a problem exists. Too often, individuals become so absorbed by the routines of work or the habitual processes that govern their working lives that they fail to ask themselves if work is still interesting or stimulating.

Three or four times a year, evaluate the level of interest you have in your job. If that level is found wanting, consider implementing some of the suggestions we make below. As a corollary, we should add that if you are bored, you must take personal responsibility for overcoming your boredom. If you believe that your current level of boredom is inherent to your job and thus cannot be removed, then your conviction may come to pass. While there are routine or dull aspects of virtually all jobs, boredom is generally a personal matter, and it is up to you to remove it.

Determine Precisely the Reason(s) for Your Boredom. If you are to overcome boredom, you must first determine its cause or causes. Simply saying, "Oh, it's just everything at work" or "I'm not sure what it is" will do little to help you resolve the problem. Become a detective and search for the true causes of your workplace boredom. We hope the following suggestions will help you in your search.

1. Create a Boredom Log. This is nothing more than charting in a log (diary) those activities that you find stimulating and those that you find dreadfully dull. Indicate in your log the intensity of stimulation or boredom that you experience with each activity and any contextual information. Contextual information—whether you slept poorly the night before, are experiencing stress in your personal life, or may be excited about an upcoming vacation—is important for accurately identifying the *true reasons* for your boredom. It is easy, for instance, to confuse boredom with fatigue or a "down" mood. Similarly, boredom over performing a typically dull task for two weeks could be masked by a vacation that you are looking forward to in the near future. Understanding the context for your boredom will help you analyze and understand precisely what is boring to you.

2. Look for patterns. After you have monitored yourself for several weeks, examine your data to see if any patterns emerge. You may note, for example, that you tend to be bored at meetings but are highly stimulated when preparing for or making a sales presentation.

3. Analyze your activities. This is key to your self-diagnosis. First, examine the activities that stimulate you and try to determine what needs within you those activities are fulfilling. If, for instance, you felt stimulated while preparing for and delivering a sales presentation, it may be because that activity fulfilled your need to perform, to be on stage, to persuade, to be creative, to be interacting with people. Second, examine your boring activities and try to

determine what needs are *not* being met. Are you bored at meetings, for instance, because you desire recognition but rarely contribute to group discussions out of shyness or fear of making a mistake? Attempting to overcome these problems by gradually participating in discussions should make attendance at meetings more stimulating. Self-awareness, determining the intensity and context of boredom, and accurate diagnosis of why you are bored are the fundamental steps in reenergizing your job and yourself. Such self-awareness will also help you to effectively apply our recommendations below.

Reenergize Your Job

Minimize Repetition and Routine and Maximize Change. All jobs have routine and repetitive aspects. The objective is not to let those aspects reach the point where they become a debilitating problem for you. The following suggestions may help you achieve this objective:

- If you are able to determine your workplace schedule, balance routine and repetitive tasks with work that you find creative, stimulating, satisfying, or unusual. Save certain types of work that you enjoy, such as meeting clients, as rewards for doing the drudgery of paperwork.
- Whenever possible, avoid scheduling an entire morning or afternoon with dull or routine work.
- Whenever possible, shuffle the order, break the patterns, and change the locations in which you do routine work.
- Reward yourself outside of work for doing a boring job. If you know you have mind-deadening tasks to do in the morning, reward yourself by having lunch at a restaurant instead of dining from a brown paper bag. If you anticipate a boring afternoon, make arrangements for meeting friends or going shopping immediately after work.
- Some may find it helpful to schedule routine or repetitive work at the end of the day. Doing rote work when you are mentally fatigued may be a happy wedding of task and ability. Still

others may find the reverse to be true. In one case, a manager scheduled boring meetings first thing in the morning. This allowed him to stay awake during the task. In the afternoon, when he was physically tired, the stimulation of interesting work kept him going.

- Determine if all of the routine and repetitive tasks that you do are genuinely necessary. Do you have to attend, for instance, as many meetings as you do? Do you have to make as many telephone calls as you do? Could your current load of paperwork be reduced?

- If possible, schedule routine and repetitive tasks at a time when colleagues have similar tasks to perform. Misery does love company, and sometimes company can make the time pass more quickly. In one organization, employees had the less-than-thrilling weekly task of applying hundreds of mailing labels on envelopes. They did this job as a group and referred to it as "social time." They talked about weddings, families, sports, and each other as they worked, and an otherwise boring job was made much more tolerable.

- Schedule an appropriate number of work breaks when doing routine or repetitive tasks.

- When someone is absent from work, ask your boss if you can cover his or her area of responsibility for the day. Ask if you can occasionally swap your routine and repetitive tasks with a colleague. At Disney World in Orlando, Florida, for instance, employees at a given attraction often rotate jobs with one another every 20 minutes.

- Whenever necessary, invoke an idea we presented in our book, *Working It Out: Sanity and Success in the Workplace*: STLFT— Something To Look Forward To. Thoughts of a wonderful weekend, a vacation, gardening, golfing, tennis, attending a play or recital, reading, or simply having time to yourself— whatever floats your boat—are mental antidotes to dreary tasks. They allow you to focus momentarily on something pleasant and serve as reminders that routine is only a small segment of a much larger canvas.

S-T-R-E-T-C-H: Reach Beyond Your Grasp. Robert Browning wrote a poem in 1855 in the voice of the Italian Renaissance painter Andrea del Sarto. Andrea is a technical genius who has thoroughly mastered the techniques of painting; in fact, he is called "The Faultless Painter." As a result he is completely bored with painting and with life. In a moment of self-reflection, he describes the source of his languor: "A man's reach must exceed his grasp,/ Or what's a heaven for?"

Those sentiments are no less relevant today. Human nature thrives on challenges. Undertaking a task whose outcome is unknown or setting goals that you are not sure you can attain—reaching beyond your grasp—provide excitement and interest, even passion, in a job.

If you have mastered your job and it now appears simplistic to you, or if you do not feel that your skills and abilities are being fully utilized, ask for a new or extra assignment. Often this can be accomplished within your organization by simply asking for different kinds of work. Spending some time with another colleague learning about his or her job may do the trick. A more extreme measure is to transfer to another job. Lateral moves are an extremely effective way to vary assignments and undertake new challenges while gaining additional workplace experience to round out your background. Determine if your job description could be expanded to include new and different assignments.

Welcome Positive Problems at Work. When you think of problems at work, your initial reaction may be to reach for an aspirin. Yet not all problems are negative; in fact, some add spice and taste to our jobs. Confronting and solving such problems as unmotivated employees, rising costs, declining market shares, poor publicity, and dyslexia in the classroom can keep people emotionally and intellectually alive. These are positive problems that promise to keep boredom at bay. Furthermore, solving these problems may fulfill an inner need. Instead of bemoaning all problems at work, try to see some as welcomed challenges.

Reenergizing You

Shake It Up—Avoid the Comfort of Complacency. Some individuals enjoy the comfort and safety of doing the same task over and over again; they stake out their turf, erect a barbed-wire fence around it, burrow a hole into the ground, and back into it. There is, in their realms, little room for doubt, mistake, misunderstanding, slip-ups, or anxiety. While this may provide comfort for some, for others it removes excitement, passion, and even interest from the workplace. When challenge is eliminated, boredom quickly fills the vacuum.

If you are bored because you have become too comfortable, try something new, take a reasonable risk, set additional goals. Determine if there are new areas to explore within your unit; ask your superior if there are ideas that he or she has thought about but has not implemented for fear of an unknown outcome; ask him or her if you may vary the procedures that you use to achieve a goal or experiment with alternative ways of doing your work.

Overcome your reluctance for trying something new and different; put to rest your fear of failing. One of the most significant elements attendant on trying a new task or a new procedure is the excitement generated by *not knowing* if you will be successful. With challenge comes the rush and thrill you had when you first began your current job.

"Don't Just Sit There, Do Something!" Take the Initiative in Overcoming Boredom. Instead of passively accepting the slings and arrows of outrageous boredom, take up arms and overcome it. Become proactive in recharging your batteries.

- Attending a seminar, workshop, or educational series will not only break your workplace routine, it may also provide you with new ways of viewing and accomplishing your job.
- Attend professional meetings; there is probably no better or more efficient way to acquire new and innovative ideas.
- In addition to asking your boss for more or different responsibilities or for more control over your work schedule, ask if

you can become involved to any degree in the decision-making process for your office or unit.

- If you are in sales and are bored with trotting out the same old dog-and-pony show, create new slides, dub in music on your videotape, explore ways of improving your presentations by using state-of-the-art technology.

- In one organization, the CEO had created what he called the "Tomorrow Fund." This was money that was given to employees who wished to experiment with new ideas that had the potential of being profitable to the organization. In order to have their ideas funded, employees wrote what amounted to grant proposals.

   Even if your organization does not offer the same opportunity, there is no reason why you cannot be creative and design a new product, a new production process, a new marketing strategy, or a new information system and then try to sell it to management.

- Develop a philosophy of Continuous Quality Improvement (CQI). This mind-set may stimulate you to strive to do the same task even better with each attempt. Thinking about CQI, strategizing on how to implement CQI, can insert stimulation into many otherwise dull and boring jobs.

Balance Boredom at Work with Stimulating Activities Outside of the Workplace. Thoughts of how you will spend your free time, as we noted earlier, provide a momentary mental escape at work, something to look forward to. In a larger sense, pleasurable activities—play—in your private life may also provide the excitement and fulfillment that is missing in your work.

   The pursuit of play is a valuable antidote to the boredom blues. Pursuing activities that you find enjoyable, such as sports, reading, working on political campaigns, listening to music, attending the theater, coaching, volunteer work, church activities, or hobbies, should give balance and verve to your life while placing you in control of your emotional well being. Play can also provide you with a sense of self-efficacy and self-esteem that may compensate for the disappointments experienced at work. Finally, play serves as a reminder that you are a human being and not a mere robot who is switched on and off at the beginning and end of each work day. Play—adult play—helps to put you in touch with what is vital and vibrant within you. It encourages you to take a chance, to act boldly, to color *outside* of the lines.[1]

"Do not suffer life to stagnate," wrote Samuel Johnson, the English lexicographer who suffered from periodic bouts of melancholia throughout his adult life, "it will grow muddy for want of motion: commit yourself again to the current of the world."

Enlist the Help of Others.   Although the primary responsibility for overcoming boredom rests squarely on your shoulders, your boss and coworkers may be able to make useful recommendations. Negative emotions such as boredom do exist, and there is little point in denying, suppressing, rationalizing, or harboring them. If politically possible, share with your colleagues the fact that you feel bored at work. Since they are familiar with both your personal predilections and the structure and culture of your work setting, they may be able to suggest practical options. You may also find that what you thought was a unique problem is, in reality, shared by many.

Since boredom is often contagious and may be contracted from comatose colleagues, make a point of spending time with coworkers who are energetic and enthusiastic, vital and vibrant, about their work and life in general. If they are engaged in dull tasks similar to yours, learn the coping mechanisms that they employ.

"Traveling Can Be More Fun than Arriving." Value the Process and Not Merely the Product.   We traditionally achieve a sense of satisfaction upon completing a task. While achieving a goal may be highly enjoyable, the means to that end, the process that leads to the product, is what is often seen as boring. We wish to encourage you, however, to value the process as well as the product, to see

---

1. For additional comments on the importance of play in our working lives, see Chapter 9, "Workhealth and Workplay," as well as our book *From Campus to Corporation and the Next Ten Years* (Hawthorne, N.J.: Career Press, 1990), pp. 164–66.

the means as well as the end as exciting and satisfying. It is the process that challenges your thinking, requires you to take chances, forces you to learn from your mistakes; it is the process that is at once engaging, difficult, intriguing, frustrating, absorbing, and infuriating.

We talked to a successful Wall Street broker who confessed: "Making $300,000 a year and having a wraparound window in the Trade Center is definitely enjoyable. But getting here was much more fun. Working for a goal I had fantasized about without any idea of whether it was realistic, dying on the phone while a client made up his mind to buy or not, trying to sell my way out of a small town—those were the things that made life exciting."

If you change your mind-set to value the process as well as the product, you may see, for example, the steps that go into a successful sales campaign—the demographic study, articulating with other offices, creating advertising copy, studying production capabilities, coordinating a staff, calling on clients—not as boring but rather as having an intrinsic interest and enjoyment.

If you change your mind-set, you may enjoy the process of waxing and polishing your car as much as having it sparkle in the sunlight, learning how to hit a tennis ball as much as serving an ace, burning the proverbial midnight oil as much as being promoted.

"Your Job Matters." Recognize and Believe in the Importance of What You are Doing. Employees who believe that their work is important, that what they are doing genuinely matters, are generally less likely to experience boredom on the job than people who have little goal satisfaction.[2]

One major problem in recognizing the importance of your work is that in a bureaucratic workplace, it is often difficult to achieve a sense of ownership. As tasks are broken down into smaller and smaller components, you may find that you are responsible for only one part or segment of a project or product and lack a holistic

---

2. See J.R. Hackman, and G.R. Oldham, *Work Redesign* (Reading, Mass.: Addison-Wesley Pub., 1980).

view of how your efforts articulate with the work of other units and other personnel. To achieve and maintain a sense of accomplishment, personal identification, and pride in what you are doing, learn the operational dynamics of your firm. This may be done by having your boss provide you with an overview, reading company publications, or touring company facilities. Since firms change directions and dynamics, your sense of how you fit into the larger organizational picture should be personally updated periodically. These steps should help you see the significance of what you do.

In one company, an employee's job was to stamp identification numbers on returned surveys. To counteract what the manager knew could be a terribly dull and tedious task, she took the time to show the employee why his job was so crucial. She described the chaos that would emerge if an identification number was mistakenly duplicated or if the sequence was disrupted. She explained how the number was at the heart of the survey location and retrieval system. She gave meaning, and with it a degree of stimulation, to the employee's job. Unfortunately, many managers are not this wise. Take the initiative to learn of the importance of what you do.

"It's What You Do that Counts." Protect Your Intrinsic Satisfaction with a Passion. Intrinsic satisfaction—the fulfillment and enjoyment you experience from your work that derives from the nature of the work itself—is a vital element in job satisfaction and the avoidance of boredom.

Unfortunately, we sometimes unwittingly permit extrinsic rewards—rewards derived from sources outside of the task—to detract from our intrinsic satisfaction.[3] Extrinsic rewards such as salary, a company car, a year-end bonus, and a large office may create a smoke screen that prevents you from recognizing the intrinsic merit and value of what you are doing. When employees look at their jobs largely as means of gaining extrinsic rewards, they may minimize or simply not notice the true importance of their work and hence may lose interest in it.

---

3. S.T. Fiske, and S.E. Taylor, *Social Cognition.* (New York: Random House, 1984).

There are several steps you may take to remain mindful of the intrinsic importance of what you are doing:

• Think about the *consequences* of your work—the people who are affected by what you do, the chain of events that takes place because of you. Review the intrinsic value of your work on an ongoing basis.

• Remind yourself of the importance of what you do by carefully observing the reactions of the people you serve. A waiter or waitress may, over months and years, become blind to the smiles on the faces of his or her customers; a bus driver may no longer hear the compliments of passengers picked up on a rainy morning; an insurance agent may forget the sigh of relief from a nervous client calling after a $600 fender bender.

• Reflect periodically on the personal pride and sense of fulfillment you experience when you do your job well.

• If you are a manager, spend some time helping members of your staff identify their intrinsic rewards.

Making Good Decisions

Select a Job that Is Interesting to You.   Our final recommendation is also our first recommendation. Practice preventive medicine; avoid the problem of boredom by selecting a job that you find exciting and fulfilling, a type of work that will spark you to approach each day and each task with enthusiasm. Ralph Waldo Emerson suggested the importance of personal interest 150 years ago when he wrote, "Nothing great can be achieved without enthusiasm." Enthusiasm motivates you to rise early in the morning and to work late at night; it helps you to overcome the routine and predictable elements of all jobs instead of being overcome by them.

The importance of selecting a job in which you have a personal and professional interest was underscored by a poll conducted in 1987 by *USA Today.* Workers in a broad sample of occupations were asked what they believed was the most vital element in their jobs. Thirty-nine percent, the largest group, responded that job satisfaction was the single most important ingredient in looking for a job and in maintaining interest in it.

In selecting a job, it is important not to be deluded by superficial matters. Separate the accoutrements of a job—a lengthy title that makes you sound like you are a heartbeat away from the presidency, an expense account, a company car—from the essence of the position. To base a job selection on appearance, perks, and peripherals is to court potential boredom and ennui; to base a job selection on the love you have for a certain type of work is to court happiness and fulfillment.

Selecting a job that suits the individual is so important, in fact, that we believe personnel directors and anyone who hires job applicants should make a "boredom declaration" to all candidates. Such a declaration would forewarn applicants about any possibly boring aspects of the jobs they are seeking so that each would be able to make a more informed decision about whether a given job is right for him or her.

Stop Hoping! If All Measures Fail, Leave a Boring Job.   If you find that the level of boredom you are experiencing at work is intolerable; if you believe that it is seriously affecting your emotional, psychological, or physical well being, and if all attempts to alleviate the boredom have failed, then there is little recourse except to change jobs.

Changing jobs provides an excellent opportunity to learn more about yourself. Analyze why you found your job boring; list the precise elements of it that became insufferable to you. Evaluate new positions carefully; look at the daily realities that may lie hidden beneath surface glitz and glamour; examine the culture of the firm, the types of people with whom you will be working, and the variety of tasks you will perform. Compare the goals and objectives of a potential employer with what you find professionally satisfying. Compare the potentially boring aspects of a new job with your list of spirit-killing elements that made you flee from your last one.

Honest introspection and precise analysis may not insure infallible choices, but they should help you to avoid making the same mistake twice.

THE POSITIVE SIDE TO BOREDOM

While it may seem improbable at first blush, your workplace boredom may actually be a blessing. Boredom is often an emotional and psychological alarm clock that awakens you from lethargy and tells you there are parts of you that are crying out to be realized and fulfilled. It can let you know that you have mastered your job and that it is time to start anew. It can let you know that you have changed, that you have grown, and that what satisfied you in the past no longer seems sufficient. It is a vivid reminder that you are not a petrified creature with static interests but rather are a vital, growing, developing person with evolving interests. It can let you know that it is time for self-discovery, time to strip away illusions and determine what really makes you tick. It can be a signal to your mind and emotions that it is time to take reasoned risks, to struggle, to commit; it is a signal that you are ready for new challenges, new horizons, new beginnings, and new dreams, "to seek, to strive, to find," according to Tennyson's *Ulysses*, "and not to yield."

Chapter Four

The Problems of Success I

I Wish I Were Successful

Steve M. had been working in corporate sales for 10 years. While his career progress was respectable— one promotion and average salary increases—he had expected to be much further along at age 35. Several coworkers with equal longevity were on the fast track, receiving more promotions, larger merit raises, and greater responsibilities, and he could not understand why their successes eluded him. "I meet my deadlines, never miss a meeting, discharge all my responsibilities, and receive positive feedback from my boss; why are they more successful?" Confused and annoyed, he was on a golden treadmill, working well at a job that he enjoyed but unable to scale the corporate ladder as rapidly as he wished. As his frustration increased, he began to dread Monday mornings and work in general: "In school I knew what to do to succeed; at work I haven't been able to find the formula. I can't stand working this way."

Susan S. was a huge success by anyone's standards. Hard work, intelligence, ambition, and tenacity had combined for a career that included two vice presidencies of Wall Street brokerage firms, a trusteeship of a small liberal arts college, and membership on several boards of directors—all by age 42. Yet Susan was miserable with her achievements. "They are all the result of dumb luck. I really did not legitimately earn any of these positions; I just got the breaks. I die a hundred times each day worrying that someone will find out that I am a fraud, that I am not smart, and that I really don't deserve what I have gotten. I am worried that my secretary will find out, and I am petrified at meetings that the next time I open my mouth my secret will be known."

Susan S. was experiencing a common problem among high achievers. Often the most successful people—the individuals you would be convinced have the most confidence in themselves—honestly believe that their success is a fluke, a series of lucky breaks. This type of behavior is so common, in fact, that psychologists have given it a name: The Impostor Phenomenon.

Americans have had a love affair with success since the late 1800s, the Gilded Age, the heyday of Andrew Carnegie, John D. Rockefeller, and J. P. Morgan. Success for these czars of capitalism was part of our manifest destiny; its value and merit were never questioned.

The American belief in and fascination with success is still very much in evidence. Television talk shows and radio interview shows, which were once the exclusive preserves of Hollywood celebrities having their 15 minutes of fame, are now increasingly populated by the barons of the business world, tycoons, and entrepreneurs. Programs such as "Lifestyles of the Rich and Famous" have created new types of celebrities: people who have made it in the workplace and the board room.

When we are not watching people who have attained success, we are reading about it, taking seminars on how to achieve it, or lamenting our fate for letting it elude us. The advice we are given for reaching its heady, oxygen-depleted heights ranges from the sane—work hard—to the inane: arrive late for lunch, use a foreign phrase every now and then, wear a red power tie, have yourself paged at a restaurant, answer a difficult question with another question, and let people know you have a lover. If Machiavelli were alive today, he would be embarrassed at his naïveté.

It should not be surprising that our national love affair with success has caused widespread frustration and distress among workers. We are constantly being reminded of the importance of success; we are surrounded by advertisements for the symbols of success; we are frequently given the message that we cannot be happy unless we are successful. Yet, for most mere mortals, success is just beyond our reach. We find ourselves in a frustrating position akin to that of Tantalus, the king in Greek mythology who was condemned to stand chin-deep in water with fruit-laden branches hanging just above his head, yet was unable to reach either food or drink.

While being unable to achieve success causes much of the working public to feel anxious, so too does being successful. It may seem ironic to those who are struggling to get up the ladder that people already in the aerie also dread Monday mornings. For many, success has been accompanied by disillusionment and disappointment. Rather than being a panacea, success has left them with a hollow, empty feeling or one of increased fear that it and all that it has brought will suddenly, mysteriously vanish. In some cases we shall examine, the dream of success has even turned into a nightmare.

We shall discuss in this chapter and the next the problems of success from both vantage points. For those who, like Steve M., are frustrated because they seem to be on a treadmill, plodding away but getting nowhere, we wish to offer several recommendations for becoming successful in the workplace, or at least for giving your career a boost. These recommendations, unlike many that you may be accustomed to hearing and reading, stress *substance* rather than *style*, *matter* rather than *method*.

One of the worst feelings about work is wanting to be successful and not having a clue about how to realize your goal. We wish to remove the doubt and uncertainty and provide you with a rudder and a map.

For those who dread Monday mornings because success has turned out to be bittersweet, vacuous, unfulfilling, or even, as in the case of Susan S., depressing, we shall discuss how to overcome these negative feelings and enjoy the fruits of your labor.

HOW TO ACHIEVE SUCCESS IN
THE WORKPLACE

The race does not always go to the swiftest; nor does the contest always go to the strongest. But that is the way that I am betting.

We live in a culture that stresses being number one, being first, being top dog. It should not be surprising that success is often defined in these terms and that workers feel unhappy if they are not number one. We wish to suggest, however, that success is a personal concept and that its definition has more to do with one's expectations and goals than it does with being number one. For some, success is becoming a CEO; for others, it is getting an initial promotion; for still others, it is simply getting a job. If you have achieved your goals, if you have met your expectations, then you are successful, and the feelings of fulfillment and satisfaction that you are experiencing are inextricably linked to your achievement.

If you believe, however, that your goals and expectations are not being fulfilled; if you, for instance, wish to be promoted, to rise through the ranks, or to be given ever-greater responsibilities and salary and you are not achieving any of these objectives, then we wish to offer several recommendations that may help give direction and efficacy to your career. While these recommendations may not cure all of the problems that you face at work, they form, we believe, the basis for individual success in the workplace.

The Success Equation

$$\text{TASK INTEREST} + \text{GOAL SATISFACTION} = \text{JOB AND CAREER SUCCESS}$$

As we have noted in past books,[1] the most important single piece of advice we can give for achieving success in the workplace is to select a job that is inherently interesting to you, with goals that are challenging and satisfying. *Task interest* means choosing a job that you find exciting and fulfilling, a job that fits your personality

---

1. "The Success Equation" along with brief parts of this chapter, first appeared in *From Campus to Corporation and the Next Ten Years* (Hawthorne, N.J.: Career Press, 1990).

and is enjoyable for you, a job that allows you to grow and develop professionally and personally. It is more likely that you will achieve success at a job that fulfills your dreams and sparks you to approach each day and each responsibility with enthusiasm than at a job for which you feel colossal indifference or only mild interest.

Goal satisfaction is both a process and an outcome; it is the result of the pleasure you derive from working toward a goal *and* the gratification you receive from attaining it. Since success is goal related, it is in your own best interest to pursue goals that are meaningful to you and reflect your values. One way of identifying such goals is to answer the question, "When I retire and look back on my career, what will I wish to say that I have accomplished?"

The following guidelines may help you create an appropriate success equation:

You First.   Define the elements of the success equation to reflect your values, your predilections, your dreams, and your desires. Do not let family and friends define task interest and goal satisfaction for you; only you can determine them.

No Gimmes.   Select a job whose goals are challenging but attainable by you. It is of little profit to toil at a job for which you are ill-suited and thus at which you will probably not achieve success. Jobs for which you are physically unsuited are generally obvious: if you are 5'6" tall and feel as though you need CPR after climbing a flight of stairs, it is not realistic to try to play professional basketball. Jobs for which you may be emotionally or temperamentally unsuited, however, are not always as obvious. The key is to maximize the person–job fit. Make an honest self-assessment of your strengths and weaknesses, your skills and deficiencies, your predilections and aversions. You may find it useful to make a list of them and a list of the attributes, talents, and psychological factors required of a specific job to see if you have a successful person–job match.

Breathe Deeply and Relax.   Be patient. Not everyone knows what job or career he or she wishes to pursue at an early age. Do not let this bother you; careful and thoughtful introspection and planning takes time and effort. The time and effort you expend, however, may help you avoid false job and career starts.

Remember Gumby. Be flexible. Allow your success equation to evolve and even change as you and your life change. Adhering rigidly to a definition of success that is no longer meaningful or relevant to you will most likely result in frustration and disquiet, even though you may have achieved success.

The success equation is affective as well as effective. Task interest and goal satisfaction translate into a feeling that you, your job, and your career are in balance and feel right.

Learn Your Job Thoroughly and Perform It With Excellence

Advancement in the workplace is primarily based on the quality of your job performance. If the quality of your work has been merely adequate or mediocre, it is unrealistic to expect your boss to elevate you to a more demanding and complex job. It is imperative, then, to devote your time and energy to learning your job from top to bottom, side to side, and front to back, and then to do your job as well as you possibly can. All other activities at work, while not without value, should be subordinated to the bedrock of a successful career: learning and doing. As Thomas Edison succinctly put it, "There is no substitute for hard work."

The following suggestions may help you improve your job performance:

Back to Basics. Make reading a passion. Reading is one of the most effective and powerful methods for expanding your knowledge and understanding of your job, and for staying on the cutting edge. Allocate no less than four hours per week to work-related reading.

Dial 1-900-TALK. Make "work talk" a passion. We believe that one of the least-used methods of performance enhancement is talking to colleagues about your work. Discuss all aspects of what you are doing—your assumptions, approaches, methods, problems, evaluations, future plans—and solicit feedback from coworkers. Be proactive; approach them rather than waiting for them to ask you about your work. Not only may your colleagues offer valuable suggestions, but you will also benefit from thinking through these issues.

If work talk is valuable, gossip is a deadly waste of time. One manager we knew used to spend the major portion of his day engaged in impromptu chats about office politics, romance among the filing cabinets, and who was up and who was down in the corporate stock market. He purposely left his door open, trolling for interlopers. Rarely did he talk about quality control, total quality management, or continuous quality improvement. After a year he gained the reputation of being a negative work talker; shortly after that he was looking for a new job.

The Truth, the Whole Truth, and Nothing but the Truth.   Evaluate your performance with a rigorous honesty: "Have I consistently met deadlines?" "Has the quality of my work been consistently high?" "Have I fulfilled all the requirements of my job?" "Have I met the expectations of my boss?" We also recommend that you ask yourself a bottom-line question: "If I were a manager, would I promote me?"

Wear Tasteful Billboards.   Make your achievements, skills, and abilities visible in a tasteful fashion. Inform your boss about projects that have gone well, ideas you have for improved productivity and efficiency in your unit, and professional training that you are receiving. Subtle and diplomatic self-marketing is not out of place.

While following these suggestions and learning how to do your current job well, identify and develop the skills and abilities that you will need to perform the job at the next higher echelon. Although higher management will be most concerned over the quality of your present work, they may also wish to see if you have developed the skills and abilities needed for advancement. Hence, if the next-higher job demands negotiating skills or advanced technical skills, you may wish to develop them by reading books on those topics, attending workshops, or taking classes.

Keep Yourself Motivated

Successful people are generally highly motivated. Motivation has many parents: it comes from unfulfilled personal needs, the passion that people have for their jobs, the commitment they have to their goals, the excitement of constantly being challenged, the desire to excel, and the pride they have in striving and achieving. Motivated people satisfy all their responsibilities, discharge all their duties, meet all their deadlines. Furthermore, successful people are almost always self-motivated. They are doers and believers in themselves and in their work; they do not need to be jump started with each new project or assignment.

We have several suggestions for maximizing your motivation:

Again, No Gimmes.   Seek a job that is challenging and that fully utilizes your skills, talents, and abilities. Jobs that offer simple or shallow victories will not stimulate you to achieve excellence. (It should not be surprising that this recommendation is also one of the antidotes to boredom that we suggested in Chapter Three.)

Look Inside the Box.   Stress and focus on the intrinsic rewards of your job. Focus on the rewards you are receiving from the work itself, the satisfaction you feel from completing a difficult task, the fulfillment you experience from being productive, the good feeling you get from knowing that you are making a valuable contribution to your firm and its clients. Too often individuals allow extrinsic rewards (salary and promotion) to distract them from the intrinsic merits and enjoyment of what they are doing.

Sleep on a Different Side of the Bed.   Experiment with change. Try new approaches to your work; experiment when appropriate with innovative techniques and fresh methods for solving problems and completing projects. Bring creativity to your workplace life. It is difficult to maintain a high level of motivation when you are engaged in habitual patterns.

Sandbox Time.   Schedule play activities with the same degree of commitment that you schedule work activities. It is difficult to maintain a high level of motivation without recharging your batteries with play.

Learn the Culture of Your Firm and Conform to It

Companies, like people, have unique and distinctive personalities. If you wish to succeed in a specific organization, it is necessary to learn and adopt its specific modes of acceptable and unacceptable behavior, likes and dislikes, sacred cows and taboos.

We have four suggestions for helping you learn the culture of a firm:

Look It Up!   Be a careful and attentive researcher. The culture and personality of a firm are revealed in seemingly endless ways. Bulletin board announcements of training seminars may indicate a corporate culture that values education and keeping on the cutting edge. Notices about social events or team sports may suggest that participation in group activities and socializing outside of work are the norm. Sparsely decorated offices and corridors may suggest a frugal, no-nonsense corporate philosophy. An abundance of pictures and wall decorations and plush furniture may denote a firm that values warmth, conviviality, and symbols of success. Desks in offices placed between the visitor and the employee may suggest a degree of formality and conservatism that one would not sense in offices in which desks are placed against the walls, thereby removing any physical barrier between the visitor and the employee. Part of being a good researcher, we hasten to add, is to collect a sufficient amount of data before drawing conclusions.

The Present Is Always a Rediscovery of the Past.   Be an astute historian; the more things change, the more they stay the same. The history of a firm will often reveal the bases for many of its current practices, attitudes, beliefs, and values. Employees who have been with the organization for many years are valuable sources for oral traditions.

Adjust Your Bifocals. Study management practices. Learn as much as you can through observation and questions about the management philosophy of your firm: What motivates management's decisions? Is there a discernible way they approach problems? What do they look for in their employees? What are their likes and dislikes?

And the Winner Is. . . . Study the reward system of your firm. If you can determine the behaviors, achievements, and attitudes that are rewarded, you will have a solid understanding of your firm's norms and acceptable modes of conduct, as well as their bêtes noires.

Reading the culture and personality of a firm and learning what a company values and abhors are crucial to achieving success in that company. Your understanding of corporate culture will provide guidance for your professional and personal activities and interactions as well as increase your sensitivity to and understanding of why people and organizations act in certain ways.

Make Things Happen

Successful people generally have a take-charge attitude; they make things happen instead of waiting for them to happen. They are proactive to a situation rather than reactive. We have several recommendations for making things happen at work:

Don't Just Sit There, Do Something. Look for what needs to be done or suggest a course of action to your boss instead of waiting to be told what has to be done.

Speak Up, Please. Do not wait to be asked for your opinion; offer it in a diplomatic and professional manner. If your suggestion is not followed, do not let that wound your pride or deter you from offering future recommendations.

Swing From the Heels. When a difficult task arises, declare immediately, "Why not me?" instead of "Why me?"

Color Outside of the Lines. Develop an entrepreneurial spirit. Become willing to go beyond what is expected, to take reasonable risks, to help your firm in ways not enumerated in your job description, and to work however long it takes to complete an assignment. Volunteering to undertake a major project for top management, to wine and dine an important client, to present a report in a public forum, or to write an in-house newsletter will demonstrate your initiative while keeping you tactfully and tastefully visible to your superiors.

Learn the Reward System in Your Organization

All organizations have a formal reward system; to be successful or promoted, you must fulfill the requirements of that system. These requirements are generally easy to identify: they may be communicated to you verbally by your boss, especially in annual goal-setting sessions, expressed in your letter of appointment, or contained in company personnel publications.

Many firms, however, also have an *informal* or unstated reward system that is equally influential. Generally, the criteria of the informal or unstated reward system are more difficult to identify. In academia, for instance, one is often told that promotion depends on excellence in both teaching and publishing. While that may be the official policy for promotion, the reality is that at many institutions, teaching is not as important as publishing. In law firms the formal reward system may value excellence in legal research or courtroom presentation, but in reality the failure to attract new clients to the firm may prevent one from becoming a partner.

We are not recommending that you ignore the formal reward system; in fact, we urge you, first and foremost, to satisfy all of the formal criteria for promotion. We are suggesting, however, that you also carefully identify the informal or unstated achievements that define high job performance—and thus success—in your organization. We hope the following recommendations will help you identify them:

Learn the Why Behind the What. Analyze *why* promotions and important assignments are given. Observe the achievements and behaviors of individuals who are promoted or given key assignments. Are any of their achievements and behaviors not covered by the formal criteria for reward? If so, you have probably identified some of the informal criteria.

Talk to the Vets. Ask employees who have been with the firm for a substantial period of time for their perceptions of the informal criteria for advancement.

Learn to Read Invisible Ink. The informal reward system is a part of the culture of a firm. Learning that culture, as we suggested earlier, is vital to your success. Listening to the remarks of various managers, watching carefully the events transpiring around you, and asking questions are prudent steps in learning both your firm's culture and informal reward system.

If, after assiduously trying to accept or work with the formal and informal reward criteria of an organization, you find that you cannot assent to or believe in those criteria, we suggest that you find a job in an organization that shares your values and philosophy. You are most likely not going to succeed at your current job.

Overcome the Fear of Failing

While you may consider failure as the opposite of success, we wish you to consider it as one of the ingredients of success. Successful people are willing to take risks, to try out new ideas, to test new methods for completing assignments, to try new approaches, to look for new wrinkles. Any time you try something fresh, different, or innovative, however, you run the risk of making a mistake or failing; it goes with the territory. In fact, if you never have made a mistake at your job, you probably never have tried anything new, unusual, or innovative.

Failure is also a basic way of learning and growing; it can be as good a teacher as is success. Failure allows you to know yourself, to become aware of your weaknesses, eccentricities, and limitations as well as to gain insight into the requirements and pitfalls of your job. The key is to learn from your mistakes in order to avoid similar errors in the future.

We have several suggestions that may help you overcome the fear of failing:

Gather Ye Rosebuds . . . and Information. Research the issue thoroughly. Fear of failure often arises from a lack of adequate information about the nature of the risk that is being taken. Learning as much as you can about an undertaking before embarking on a course of action may help you determine if the risk is reasonable.

Ask, "Will I *really* die?" Determine the consequences of your proposed course of action. Individuals often fear failure because they are uncertain about what will happen to them if they fail. This uncertainty often results in a worst-case scenario in which people imagine unspeakable indignities occurring to them if they do not succeed at a task. Speak candidly to your boss about the potential consequences and benefits of a course of action to determine if the benefits outweigh the consequences.

Swing for the Fences. As a rule of thumb, we believe that if you do fail, it is better to commit a failure of commission than a failure of omission. If you commit yourself to a new idea or activity you may strike out, but you may also hit a home run; if you refuse to try a new idea or activity because of the fear of failure, you will never know what the outcome may have been. Remember, Columbus made a mistake; he was looking for a route to the Orient.

Check It Out. If you have a new idea or a new approach and you are not sure of its appropriateness, we urge you to discuss the matter with your boss and coworkers instead of being frozen in place by the fear of failing.

Overcome the Fear of Rejection

We have talked to numerous individuals who want to be successful but who, ironically, refuse to apply for higher positions within their own or other firms. Jim B., for instance, earned a degree in computer science from a midwestern university. Upon graduation, he landed a job in the marketing office of a large computer firm. His real love, however—well known to his supervisor, colleagues, and friends—was in computer and software design. He talked about this specialty, kept abreast of developments by devouring professional literature, and attended meetings in computer and software design whenever possible. Finally, a position became available in the firm's design unit; it would have meant a promotion, more responsibility, and greater salary. Jim, however, refused to apply for the job, telling his nonplussed friends, "Well, I'm satisfied where I am, no sense in looking a gift horse in the mouth." Upon further probing, Jim also revealed that he had recently suffered rejection in his personal life and did not want to become "a two-time loser."

While various rationales are given by individuals who wish to succeed but are reluctant to apply for new positions, we believe that in many cases their reluctance or refusal is based on the fear of rejection. Some are afraid that rejection will result in a bruised and battered ego. Others are dismayed at the prospect of reviving the painful feelings they experienced when they were children and received negative judgments from parents or teachers. Still others may fear that rejection will undermine their already shaky self-esteem and self-confidence.

We wish you to consider the following ideas as antidotes to the fear of rejection.

Ego Tough.   Rejection, like failure, is part of a successful person's experience. Obviously, whenever you apply for a position or, for that matter, whenever you write a report, make a sales call, ask for a raise, make a proposal at a meeting, or even express an opinion, you are putting your ego and self-esteem on the line. The alternative, however, is to stagnate, to lead a death-in-life existence, "to let," as Samuel Johnson said, "life's waters grow muddy." Accept rejection as a predictable result of an active person's climbing the career ladder.

So What Else Is New?   You may be unaware of the extent to which you are already living with rejection. Ideas, suggestions, contracts, bids, and proposals are rejected in the workplace much more frequently than they are accepted. One home renovation businessman we interviewed told us that for every ten bids he submits, nine are rejected. According to Richard Bolles, author of *What Color Is Your Parachute*, individuals who apply for jobs advertised in newspapers and magazines are invited, on the average, to three interviews for every 100 applications. Rejection is probably nothing new to you; you have been living with it and most likely will continue to live with it.

It's Not Really You. Do not take rejection personally. Although rejection may smart a bit for even the most stoical, its sting may be mitigated if you put a negative response to a job application or a workplace activity in the proper context. Your application or your request has been rejected; you as a person—your values, attitudes, and beliefs—have not been rejected.

Cheap Tuition. Look upon a rejection as a learning experience. A rejection can help you understand what is lacking in your background, training, or experience. It is a professional evaluation that can help you to identify specific gaps and prompt you to fill them.

Keep It in Perspective. Hold the rejection out at arm's length and balance it with the many accomplishments in your professional and personal life: reflect on what you have achieved, the esteem in which your family and friends hold you, the tasks you have undertaken and successfully completed, and the skills and abilities that you possess. At worst, reflect on the fact that you have a job and have achieved a level of expertise that allowed you to think you had a realistic chance of getting a promotion.

Develop a Support Network with Your Coworkers

Professional and personal success involve your relationship with your coworkers. How well you accomplish your assignments will often depend on the degree of support you receive from your coworkers, while their friendship is a valuable ingredient in your social support network. You will need people to whom you can turn for advice or solace, vent frustrations, and talk about disappointments. Coworkers help you enjoy the mountaintops and cope with the valleys. Cultivate a trusted support system and cherish it.

There are several concepts that we believe are essential for developing a support system:

Going Both Ways.   To have a friend, of course, implies that you must also be a friend. If your colleagues are foundering, offer them help; provide advice when you think it is appropriate; be sensitive to their needs and personal characteristics; treat them with respect; and let them know that they can depend on you.

You Are Not at the Academy Awards.   Competition is often the cause for contention among coworkers. Employees sometimes feel that they are pitted against one another, which often leads to one-upsmanship, backbiting, subtle put-downs, and a chilling and tense atmosphere at work.

The fallacy behind this view of competition is thinking that your success depends on the failure of your coworkers. In reality, your success arises from your professional and personal growth and achievement, from thoroughly learning your job and doing it efficiently and effectively. The person with whom you compete should be yourself; try to improve over past performances, find better ways of completing assignments, learn how to use your time more effectively than when you were a novice, challenge yourself to excel in the future.

Spin a Network of Support.   Your support system should extend beyond your office or firm. Join professional associations and attend professional or trade conventions and conferences for additional contacts. The individuals you will meet probably share many of your ambitions, doubts, problems, and anxieties. They are often excellent listeners to concerns that you do not wish to reveal to your coworkers.

Your family should also be included in your support network. The home and the workplace are inextricably intertwined; your family or spouse should be kept fully apprised of the problems and issues you face at work, and their advice and feedback should be zealously sought.

Seek Evaluation Periodically

It is imperative to get frequent feedback on your performance at work. If it is not supplied by your immediate superior or your colleagues, request it. There is little point to working in a self-deluded world, to thinking that you are doing well when, in reality, your work is only mediocre. Honest appraisal of your work and constructive suggestions for improvement are vital to a successful career.

If your evaluations are positive and you wish to be promoted, let that desire be known. While we do not recommend circulating audio cassettes announcing your availability for an executive suite, we believe there is absolutely nothing to be gained by remaining a silent stoic waiting to be discovered. There are times when tasteful boldness and assertiveness are entirely appropriate.

Think in Lateral as well as Vertical Terms

Success is traditionally thought of in vertical terms; you prepare yourself for the next promotion, the next assignment of increasing responsibility, the next step up the ladder.

In the current workplace environment, however, success often depends on thinking in lateral terms. It is frequently necessary to ask for help, formally or informally, from colleagues working in other offices or units, to enlist the support of people not directly involved in your specific project or assignment, to test ideas on a variety of people not in your chain of command. To complete the difficult and complex tasks assigned to you may demand coalition building, collaboration, and teamwork among colleagues of different reporting lines. Establishing and maintaining congenial relationships laterally in an organization or profession is essential if you wish to move vertically.

Senior management tends to like people who can coordinate activities across departmental lines. A major complaint among many high-level managers is that employees and managers cannot see beyond the needs of their individual units or departments.

To avoid myopia and to increase your peripheral vision, we recommend the following steps:

Walk in Someone Else's Shoes.   Job share. Spend half a day in a colleague's department learning about the challenges and problems that he or she faces.

Oh, So That's What You Do.   Attend training sessions that focus on issues confronting lateral departments or that deal with topics that cut across organizational lines.

Swim in Other Pools.   Volunteer to work on committees or projects that involve staff from other departments. This is also a valuable way to expand your workplace network.

Walk and Talk.   Share information about your job and department with staff from other departments. This can often be done in social settings such as lunch, dinner, or recreational activities.

Get Wired.   Ask other departments to put you into their communications loop.

Meet New People.   Initiate activities, such as brown bag lunches, in which colleagues from a variety of departments can discuss issues that are both common and unique.

Not only is it vital to be able to work with people across organizational lines, but it may also be advisable to make lateral career moves if they can provide you with additional training or experience. Many successful people, for instance, work in sales for several years and then move into a marketing position in order to expand their repertoires of skills and abilities. In effect, such people are positioning themselves for a vertical move.

Give Yourself Time for Play

If play is, as we suggested in Chapter Three, an important activity for avoiding boredom, it is also crucial to preserving one's sanity and equanimity. Thus it serves a vital function in achieving success in the workplace.

Play allows people to decompress after work, to purge themselves of pent-up emotions and hostility, to let the steam out of the pressure cooker. It gives them a respite from their responsibilities and provides them with the peace and calm needed to reflect on their goals, achievements, and relationships.

Play can also offer working people a sense of personal control and individual effectiveness, a sense that they are attaining desired goals when those needs are not being met at the workplace. If, for instance, you do not receive a promotion you desperately desire, you may compensate for some of that disappointment by being elected to the presidency of a local civic association or booster club.

Finally, play serves as a reminder that we are thinking, feeling organisms possessing creativity, passion, curiosity, and spontaneity. These characteristics are plentiful in children—as the poet William Wordsworth reminds us, we come into this world "trailing clouds of glory"—but in our adult world they are quickly replaced by routine, boredom, and predictability. Life, Wordsworth continues, "is but a sleep and a forgetting." In the workplace, the result of losing our sense of creativity, passion, curiosity, and spontaneity is that we too willingly rely on old solutions to new problems, apply timeworn theories to current issues, resist tackling major projects or taking risks, pour ancient wine into modern bottles— activities that are inimical to success.

While play is pursued most frequently away from the workplace, we have several suggestions for incorporating play into your working life:

Try Something Else on the Menu.   Try different approaches to standard activities. Instead, for instance, of holding staff meetings at noon on Fridays, conduct them at the end of the day and then go as a group to dinner, a play, or a night sporting event. You may also wish to experiment with holding meetings outside of your workplace.

It's All Right to Smile.   Do it with humor. Laughter is a wonderfully healthy activity to pursue. Placing cartoons on a bulletin board, circulating humorous anecdotes, or hiring a clown to celebrate someone's birthday can brighten anyone's day.

Grab a Lampshade. Be spontaneous. Often our first thoughts are our best thoughts. If you have the impulse to hold a party to celebrate landing a major account or completing a dreary project, do it.

Look Upon Learning as a Lifelong Process[2]

Since the technological leaps, complex changes, and explosion in knowledge that have occurred in virtually every field will continue at an even greater rate in the future, it is incumbent upon anyone who wishes to be successful in the workplace to pursue a variety of continuing education programs throughout his or her career. We wish to make several recommendations about how to stay abreast of the latest developments in your field.

Teach Yourself. Read voraciously. Subscribe to several professional journals and newsletters in your field. Since the lag time between the submission of a manuscript and its publication in a journal is generally less than one year, the articles or essays you read will often reflect the most current thinking in your specialty. Even the advertisements can help to keep you up-to-date.

We also recommend that you visit your local bookstore at least once a month to browse through the sections most closely related to your interests. Try to read several relevant books each month.

Let Others Teach You. Attend the major conventions, conferences, or trade shows in your field. The lectures and seminars at such meetings often reflect the most current thinking. Furthermore, valuable information can be gleaned in an informal manner simply by talking to colleagues from other firms or other locales. While expanding your knowledge of a field, attendance at such meetings will also expand your professional network.

Learning from the Inside. Attend in-house training sessions. Many companies offer extensive training sessions ranging from technical topics to basic management skills.

---

2. This and the following section first appeared in our book *Transitions: Successful Strategies from Mid-Career to Retirement* (Hawthorne, N.J.: Career Press, 1990).

Let Your Fingers Do the Walking. Locate, in the absence of in-house training programs, courses that are relevant to your needs at local educational institutions. A continuing education program from a nearby college or university is an excellent place to begin filling in the gaps in your background.

Solving the Puzzle. Take courses, workshops, or seminars in areas such as data analysis, problem solving, and the design and implementation of management information systems. Problem-solving and decision-making skills are invaluable to a manager.

The Medium is the Message. Explore the learning resources at your local library. Technical and managerial information is becoming increasingly available on videotapes. Ask the reference librarian for a bibliography of videotapes and other educational or instructional materials.

Learn to Log On and Log In. Become familiar with the learning resources in your field. Knowing how to use a library, for instance, or what government agency to call for information will spare you from spending enormous amounts of time and energy collecting data that has already been gathered. Knowing how to use learning resources will help you research projects more thoroughly and identify judicious courses of action. Knowing how to use learning resources will also help you to answer questions and gather data independently; you will not have to worry that you are asking your colleagues and boss for an excessive amount of assistance.

It has been predicted that the changes in the workplace during the next decade will be even more extensive and rapid than the changes that have occurred in the past 10 years. Your ability to respond to those changes, to learn new skills and techniques, to adapt and continue to grow, will largely determine your professional success.

Technology: Be User-Friendly

It would be difficult to think of a revolution in the workplace more dramatic and influential than the changes wrought by the computer. We believe, however, that we have seen only the tip of the iceberg; the other eight-ninths will emerge in the decade ahead. Increasingly, it will be necessary for employees to conceptualize projects, methods, approaches, and desired results in terms of computers and information systems. It will be difficult, if not impossible, to remain competitive with your peers without the ability to use a computer.

If you do not have a computer in your office, ask your boss to procure one. If you do not own a personal computer, please purchase one. If you do not know how to use a computer, please learn. Enroll in a basic computer course, take a seminar or workshop on computer software, hire a private tutor to teach you, or ask your son or daughter in grammar school to instruct you.

While computers will have an obvious impact on your ability to store, sort, and retrieve information, familiarity with their capabilities will also help you to think in more creative and expansive terms about projects and problems. You will be able to create "what if" scenarios to test hypotheses, options, and approaches. You will be able to access an extraordinary range of data bases, including entire library holdings, consumer surveys, and demographic information on a vast array of markets in the United States and the world. You will be willing to undertake projects and initiatives broader in scope and more complex than you would have ever dreamed of undertaking without a computer.

The computer can also help you in one of the most essential activities in the workplace: expressing your ideas in written form clearly and cogently, precisely and persuasively. Sitting down to write with a pencil or pen in hand, revising a document by the time-worn cut-and-paste method, emending a manuscript by scribbling interlinear comments, editing by crossing out and replacing by superscript or marginalia will, we believe, resemble writing practices in the future as much as alchemy resembles science.

Writing is a process that involves thinking as well as communicating. As you write, you are simultaneously redefining your ideas, improving and clarifying, altering and modifying them. It is a process that is circular as well as linear, one in which you revise as you write, rethink as you write, and change what you have written while at the same time moving forward.

Computers are ideally suited to help you perform the simultaneous processes of writing and thinking. With a few strokes you can replace a word, change a tense, correct a mistake, modify an idea, and introduce additional material to bolster your argument. A computer allows you, with a minimum of effort, to alter or change your thesis while in the very act of expounding it. It permits you to move a sentence or paragraph from one place to another with ease, to reorder ideas, to change your emphasis, and to try out an idea just to see how it reads.

The benefits of being computer-literate extend, of course, far beyond those suggested here. Whatever time or money or effort it takes to learn how to use a computer, it will be one of the best career investments you have ever made.

Have Realistic Expectations about Promotion

It is easy to become impatient about getting promoted. You may watch your boss do his or her job and assume that you can do it equally well. While this may be true, it does not mean that you are ready for promotion. Your boss has probably been in the firm longer than you, demonstrated loyalty and commitment to the organization, proved that he or she can handle difficult assignments, and developed—through experience—a global view of how the firm operates.

Be patient and have realistic expectations about promotions and your future. Successful associates in accounting firms, for instance, struggle for upwards of six to eight years before they are made partners; physicians often do not become full-fledged members of their professional community until they are in their mid-thirties; baseball players may labor in the minor leagues for five or six years before they reach the majors; academics rarely become full professors before they are in their late forties. Measure your upward progress in the context of your firm and profession.

We have throughout this chapter limited our discussion to success in the workplace. There are, we hasten to add, various types of success. Perhaps the most significant type is more holistic than we have described. It embraces your family and personal relations, your emotional and psychological health, your feelings of happiness and well-being as well as your work. Success in the workplace at the expense of the general quality of your life is a Pyrrhic victory at best.

Achieving and maintaining success in this larger context often involves trade-offs and concessions in your professional life. We urge you to look at your life holistically and to make success in the workplace a part—not the be all and end all, not the alpha and omega—but only a part of your overall strategy for a successful and happy life.

Chapter Five
The Problems of Success II
I Am Successful, But I Am Still Miserable

When I got to Easy Street, I found it was under repair.

One more success like that, and I'll sell my body to a medical institute.
—Groucho Marx, *The Cocoanuts.*

B reak out a case of the bubbly! Strike up the band! Call a national holiday!

After years of putting your nose to the grindstone and your shoulder to the wheel (who could ever work in that position?), you have finally been promoted. Success is yours. All your wishes have been granted; you are now in the land of milk and honey; you have reached nirvana; it is raining soup, and you have a spoon.

Right?

Not always.

SUCCESS AND MISERY

Most people in the workplace have a romantic view of success. They feel it means wealth, security, extended vacations, foreign cars, independence, power, and prestige; it is the elixir that transforms the base metals of life into gold. It is a Norman Rockwell painting come to life.

Yet, for many, success more closely resembles a Franz Kafka creation. Success for them is a bitter irony. After having worked so hard and sacrificed so much to attain it, they find that success has brought to them not happiness, but a number of negative feelings: loneliness, frustration, disillusionment, stress, anxiety, fear, and even guilt.

"Success" and "negative feelings" may sound like oxymorons, like "jumbo shrimp" or "chocolate diet," but for many those words have a cause and effect relationship. In this chapter, we wish to examine some of the dominant problems brought on by success and discuss steps that may be taken to resolve the negative feelings occasioned by them. If you are one of those individuals for whom success has been bittersweet, we want to help you enjoy more fully the many benefits of your achievements.

... But Nothing Has Changed

One of the most common fallacies we have found about success is the belief that it will somehow change your life radically, and change it for the better. The truth behind that myth is that success rarely makes fundamental changes in one's life. It can, of course, bring you material comfort and a measure of prestige, but it cannot strengthen a weak marriage, resolve family problems, provide peace of mind, or bring inner contentment. If fundamental problems existed in your life before your success, they will probably continue to exist after it; in fact, your success may even exacerbate those problems.

Have a Realistic View of Success. The sense of disillusionment that many people experience after achieving success may be avoided by having a realistic view of what success can and cannot do for you. Success can have a major impact on your life-style, for it can bring you a host of creature comforts and the freedom to enjoy them. It can reduce your financial worries and provide you with some protection against the vagaries of life. Success can allow you to pursue interests that you would have neglected, to enjoy a range of experiences that would have been denied to you, to meet people whose paths you would not have crossed, and to bring you visibility that would not have otherwise occurred.

While success may have a major impact on the externals of your life, it often will have the least impact on your inner world and private life. Success does not automatically confer a sense of self-worth, self-respect, or self-esteem. If you wish to use it to prove to yourself and others that you are a worthwhile and good person, you have purchased a lifelong ticket for a treadmill. Nor does success, in and of itself, remove self-doubt or strengthen self-image; it does not automatically tame the wild beasts that roam within. It does not confer infallibility or omnipotence, nor does it suddenly make a selfish person altruistic, a brusque personality pleasant, or a negative worldview positive. It does not make children obey their parents, inundate one with worthwhile friends, or bring happiness. Addressing fundamental issues and problems involving your personality, temperament, character, or relationship with others demands introspection, self-analysis, and the courage to take resolute action.

Enjoy success for all the good things that it can bring to you, but do not look upon it as a panacea.

It "Is" Lonely At the Top

"It is lonely at the top" is a facetious statement, unless you happen to be lonely and at the top; then it is a painful description of what numerous successful people experience. While the number of one's acquaintances may increase as he or she rises in an organization or profession, we have found that the number and quality of one's friendships at work can actually decrease.

One individual with whom we spoke, Timothy R., a vice president of a financial investment house, commented in a dejected voice about his ambivalent feelings toward success: "I traveled from a small town in Texas to the big city and am now making more money each year than my father made in his lifetime. But even money can be hard to enjoy by yourself. When I started out, I had no time to socialize; in fact, I slept in my office on many nights. Now the only time I go to the theater is when I'm entertaining a client. There is no one at work that I can trust, much less befriend. Most of them are after my job, waiting like hungry sharks for me to make a mistake. Sometimes I think I would trade a little success for a night of playing poker with some good old boys."

Friends are necessary for maintaining your psychological health and emotional well-being. They are people with whom you can share personal thoughts, private fears, inner dreams and doubts, and the truth that lies beneath the surface that everyone else sees.

The successful individual, however, often finds himself or herself in a catch-22 situation: while it is important to develop personal relationships with people who understand the issues and problems you face at work—indeed, workplace friendship is one of the key elements in job satisfaction—it can be unwise to reveal too much about yourself to either subordinates or your boss. If you are to retain your authority over those who report to you, it is sometimes necessary to maintain a certain distance, which a social friendship would probably preclude. Furthermore, forming friendships with some of your subordinates may create a morale problem among the others, who may feel that your evaluation of friends would not be objective. Likewise, having heart-to-hearts with your boss may disclose too much about yourself to someone who is evaluating you for future assignments.

It is easier to form friendships with colleagues at your level yet this, too, as suggested by the remarks of Timothy R., is fraught with difficulties. If you are likely to compete with a colleague, you may not feel comfortable, nor may it be prudent, to bare your soul.

To compound the problem of loneliness, the successful individual has frequently failed to develop friendships outside of the workplace. Achieving success probably required many 16-hour workdays and working weekends, too. That may have left little time for developing personal relationships or pursuing activities with potential friends. Now that you are able to find time to socialize outside of work, you do not have a network of friends, nor do you know how or where to develop social contacts.

Connecting With Others.   The good news is that success does not have to mean loneliness. Friendships can, and should, be made at work. The problems that may make you feel uncomfortable establishing friendships with colleagues in your office should not apply to colleagues from other offices or units within your firm. While you would have much in common with them, they would not be directly in competition with you or working for you.

If you are working in a large company, meeting such individuals should not be difficult. You may wish, for instance, to volunteer to work on a variety of task forces composed of people from other offices or units. Special committees, such as in-house fund-raising groups for charitable causes, often draw individuals from a cross section of offices and reporting lines. Participation in recreational activities sponsored by your firm—sports, brown-bag discussion groups—is also an effective way to meet people. Since it is emotionally healthy to be able to share your workplace frustrations and problems with people who would have a basic understanding of them, we urge you to take the initiative to meet appropriate people in your firm.

Attending professional meetings, conferences, and conventions is another effective way to meet kindred spirits. While you have probably experienced the professional benefits of networking, there are social and personal benefits that should be explored as well. Tapping these benefits is often simply a question of context. In the past, you may have looked upon professional relationships in a purely business fashion. If, however, you look upon these relationships as having a potential social and personal dimension, you may discover a network of people very much like yourself. You may even find, for instance, that these colleagues share the problem of isolation that you are experiencing. Like a stone cast in a pond, networking sends out ever-widening ripples: the individuals that you meet through professional meetings often belong to additional networks that open the doors to even more potential social contacts.

We suggested in our discussion of how to achieve success that it is vital for individuals to balance their working lives with play. One of the beneficial aspects of play that we did not discuss was the opportunity it affords to form friendships. Participating in amateur theatrical groups, civic or political associations, school or church groups, and volunteer or fund-raising organizations is not only an excellent way to "get out of yourself," it is also an effective method to meet people who share nonprofessional interests with you.

If you had a special interest or hobby—playing a musical instrument, painting, tennis, golf, handball—before you decided to dedicate yourself to 16-hour workdays, join groups of people who have a similar interest now. You can often locate such groups by simply asking people or taking a walk through the Yellow Pages. You may also want to contact the local chapter of your college alumni association; frequently alumni groups sponsor social, recreational, cultural, travel, and educational activities. It is not, we hasten to add, a question of finding the time to pursue these activities; to maintain your workplace sanity, you can hardly afford *not* to take the time.

One last recommendation. One of the most common activities for working people is to "do lunch." Often, however, invitations sound perfunctory: "Let's have lunch sometime." "Stop by for lunch someday." "Give me a call when you're free." Luncheon dates or promises of future meetings frequently sound phony or insincere if they are left to some vague future time. If you wish to pursue a relationship, be specific. Ask the person if he or she would like to have lunch next Tuesday at one o'clock, or dinner on Friday at seven, or a drink after work tomorrow at five. In a world that is often filled with cant and affectation, offering a specific time and date lets the person know that you genuinely want to spend time with him or her.

The Loneliness of the Successful Woman

Although loneliness is a human emotion that is gender blind, it is particularly rife and profound among successful working women. While they frequently suffer loneliness in the workplace for the reasons already discussed, women are, in addition, often denied the benefits of close friendships with males and of participation in male-dominated social networks at work simply because they are women.

A number of the women we interviewed suggested that the primary problem in forming close friendships with men at work is that friendship may be perceived by others in the firm—perhaps even by the male friend—as a romantic relationship. The women we talked to were adamant in recommending that romantic relationships at work be avoided; such relationships are, according to one female executive, "career suicide." To avoid either the reality or the appearance of a romantic relationship, many of the women commented on the importance of maintaining a social and personal distance from male coworkers, especially subordinates. Susan J., an unmarried corporate vice president, told us that she constantly monitored her social distance during the workday: "For the men I manage in particular, I must make sure that I stay at arm's length (no pun intended, naturally). This isn't always easy: I like men and friendships. Just the other day a new male employee in an entry-level position came to work. He's a hunk—6' 2", deep blue eyes, and gorgeous blond hair—but I had to put my libido on hold. As it turned out, he was also interested in me. He asked another employee what my first name was. The employee responded, 'Her first name is vice president.' I get the word out, and then other employees spread it. I have no choice in the matter."

Another female executive agreed that "you have to be careful. You don't want to be accused of causing someone to be interested in you or to come on to you." By maintaining an aloofness or distance, women executives may be seen at times by their male colleagues as cold or mechanical. Commenting on a female colleague, one man said, "What do they do, wind her up at 7 A.M., send her to work, and then turn her off at 5 P.M.?"

The successful women we interviewed also commented on the difficulty, because of their gender, of becoming part of the male networking at work. According to Mary K., "There still exists an old-boys' club at work that drives me crazy. Our executive vice president is a male, and if you can't play tennis, golf, or poker with him, you will never relate to him as well as someone who does those activities." Women quickly learn that if they attempt to overcome their sense of isolation from the male network by "hunkering down" with the guys or by telling off-color jokes or acting like frustrated jocks, they are facilely labeled as unfeminine, aggressive, and, in the words of Susan J., a product manager for a Fortune 300 company, "bitchy."

Adding to the successful woman's sense of alienation is the frequent absence of mentoring relationships with senior executives, most of whom are male. The paucity of mentors is in part caused by the lower number of women at the upper rungs of the corporate ladder. While there are currently the same number of men and women in entry-level positions in major corporations, only 25 percent of middle management positions and only 1 percent of top management positions are held by women.[1]

Furthermore, if a woman has a male mentor, their relationship has the potential of being misunderstood by colleagues. If a male senior executive, for instance, takes a male employee on a business trip or to a convention or to dinner, it is perfectly acceptable, even laudable, conduct. If, however, he were to do so with a woman employee, it could supply mountains of grist for the rumor mill.

Being unable to form friendships at work because of the need to maintain one's distance, the failure to belong to the dominant network, and the absence of mentors can exact a serious psychological toll on successful women. Little wonder they often feel alone, isolated, and insecure.

Connecting without Romancing.   The measures we recommended to successful men who felt isolated at work—meeting people from other offices or units within the firm, joining a variety of community groups, and pursuing play activities with others—are applicable as well to successful women. To balance the lack of networking at work, it is especially vital for women to join professional organizations, caucuses, and special-interest groups where they will likely find other successful women who are facing similar problems. These individuals may provide significant career and social support, while their networks will help you make numerous additional contacts.

---

1. Bonnie Kantor. "Women in Management"; speech given at The Ohio State University, Spring 1987.

Although we think that forming a romantic relationship at work is a bad idea, we do not wish to imply that women should simply write off all men at work as potential friends. In fact, we want to encourage women to form friendships at work whenever it seems comfortable. This may mean taking the initiative and inviting a male colleague to lunch to discuss professional and business matters—just be sure to give a time and date.

The Compulsion to Continue

On the evening that his team captured the American League Division West championship for the third consecutive year, Tony LaRussa, the highly successful manager of the Oakland Athletics, remarked: "Winning the division was great each time. But each time you win it, there is even greater pressure on you to keep on winning, to repeat your success."

Success creates its own momentum; a successful person often expects to continue to succeed. For some, however, the pressure to continue to succeed interferes with the enjoyment of current success. LaRussa's words suggest that while he was feeling the satisfaction of a successful season, he was also experiencing pressure, and perhaps some anxiety, to continue his success. One wonders if a similar experience occurred to Bjorn Borg, who retired after five consecutive Wimbledon championships.

People who feel the pressure to continue to succeed find themselves on a treadmill of ever-increasing speed. With each new success comes not pleasure, but the burden to repeat that success again and again. We talked to a successful university professor who had won several teaching awards but felt pressure, more than satisfaction, from each one. "Some people I know would have felt good for the rest of their careers if they received one teaching award. My pleasure was short-lived, and even then it was mixed with anxiety and pressure. I kept imagining that when I entered the class the next day my students would be smugly sitting there, arms folded, smirks on their faces, saying to themselves, 'OK, let's see what's so great about you.' When I received my second award—just to prove that it wasn't a fluke—the pressure became even greater."

Not only does success compel some to continue their successes, but it may also place them under pressure to succeed in other, unrelated areas of their lives. We talked to one individual, for instance, who had a flourishing career in sales but felt pressured because of this to be a successful coach for his twelve-year-old son's Cub Scout baseball team. "If I can motivate a sales force, I should be able to motivate a bunch of kids." Instead of enjoying the experience of coaching, it became a self-imposed test of his abilities.

Smelling the Roses. If you are experiencing the problem of continuing success, we urge you to stop more often to smell the roses and to enjoy what you have worked so hard to accomplish. Instead of seeing success as one long, ongoing test for which a grade is never posted, try looking at your achievements as *discrete* experiences, each one of which should be savored and enjoyed. After completing a task, close your office door and give yourself a verbal pat on the back: "Hey, I just succeeded."

Remind yourself of your successes. Take five or ten minutes every few days to review what you have been doing well. Make a written list of your achievements over the past year so that you can readily think about each one and take pride in each. Dwell on how good you felt when you achieved an objective or goal. Nod off to sleep at night thinking about it. Let the moment and the feeling continue to live.

The pressure to continue to succeed, especially if it is self-imposed, may reflect a need to prove continuously that you really deserve the success that you have achieved. If this is the case, you may suffer from the Impostor Phenomenon (see p. 88).

Fear of Failure

Numerous successful people do not enjoy their enviable status because they are, ironically, afraid of failing. For some, this fear may be rooted in a lack of confidence or a poor self-image, in which case self-doubt subverts the good feeling of success.

For others, the fear of failing is based on the belief that if they fail they will be personally letting down an entire group of people.

This belief, we have found, may be especially apparent among women executives and managers. Women in leadership positions frequently feel that the fate of other women rests on their shoulders, that they have been given the burden of proving that women are at least as competent as men. This is especially true in companies, corporations, professions, or fields in which women do not have a long work history or in positions in which there have been few female predecessors. In these cases, there is no reservoir of credibility from which to draw if a woman should falter.

While women feel this particular type of pressure strongly, there are various groups of men that may also experience it. Minorities, for instance, often have a similar sense of obligation toward other members of their racial or ethnic group. If they fail, minority men and women reason, other members of their group may not be given the chance to succeed, or they may be indirectly responsible for perpetuating the bigotry of those who believe that minorities lack talent and ambition. To make matters worse, one successful minority administrator feared that if he failed it would call into question how he got his job in the first place: "If I goof up," he told us, "everyone will assume that I was just another affirmative-action appointment."

Putting It in Perspective.   If your fear of failure is the result of a lack of confidence or a poor self-image, we wish to reiterate the recommendations we made above for overcoming the compulsion to continue being successful. Remind yourself of your many achievements and of the esteem in which you are held by colleagues. Occasional failures are part of a successful career; keep them in perspective. (See Chapter Four, "Overcome the Fear of Failing" and "Overcome the Fear of Rejection.")

If your fear of failure arises from the mistaken and, in a sense, egocentric notion that one person carries the fate and future of an entire gender, race, or group on his or her shoulders—that one person can stymie the upward mobility of women and minorities, that one person can turn back the clock to a period of benign neglect—disabuse yourself of that belief. The fallacy, of course, is in thinking than one person can influence events in this fashion or that one person can affect the acceptance of generations yet unborn. You are ultimately responsible only for your own success or failure, no one else's. Instead of worrying about the fate of millions, dwell on the progress of your own career, the challenges you have met, and the accomplishments you have made.

Fearing failure because of the effect your failure may have on others also validates a most simplistic view of the world, a world-view that asserts that one can generalize about a large group of humanity based on the actions of a few people. People who hold that point of view would replace logic and thinking with mindless stereotyping. Stereotypes are smoke screens that direct attention away from individuals to trite, banal, and stale myths about groups; they enforce the logic of bigotry. If you fear failure because you believe you may damage job prospects for other members of your group, you are allowing yourself to become a victim of a mode of thinking and behaving for which, we suspect, you have little regard.

The Burden of Success

For some individuals, success brings with it not the many benefits that were anticipated, but the sobering and disturbing realization that what they do now affects the welfare of numerous others. The successful individual who becomes a CEO is suddenly forced to comprehend the full extent of his or her responsibilities; a single mistake could have disastrous consequences for employees, stockholders, suppliers, and customers. The successful nurse who becomes head nurse is responsible for the welfare not of a dozen patients, but of an entire floor of patients; her decisions and leadership suddenly have even greater life-and-death consequences.

Permit Yourself Some Humanity.   Such are the burdens of success. Successful people do, indeed, make mistakes, and when they do the consequences are often great. Since this is the reality that cannot be avoided, you can and must learn to live with it. Accept the fact that success does not confer infallibility, but also accept the fact that you attained your present status because of an impressive track record. You have been given greater responsibilities because of past accomplishments and future promise, not because someone thought that you were omniscient.

If you exercise reasonable care in making decisions, if they are based on accepted procedures, if decisions reflect your best judgment, then you have done all that anyone can do. The workplace is a complex, shifting, and at times enigmatic place where events may be altered by a seemingly infinite number of variables over which you have no control. Accept the limitations of being human.

The Pressure and Stress of Success

Pressure and stress may result from the experience of being successful or from the various problems of success that we have discussed. The manifestations of pressure and stress may be physical symptoms such as insomnia, severe indigestion, headaches, nausea, and fatigue, or they may reveal themselves psychologically as depression, nervousness, irritability, or anger. The fact that pressure and stress seem to have become as American as apple pie in no way diminishes the distress and dysfunction they cause.

Calming and Coming Down.   Naturally, we hope that by following our various suggestions for overcoming the problems of success, you will also diminish the degree of pressure and stress that you may be experiencing.

In addition to those recommendations, however, we believe that mental relaxation is an effective antidote to pressure and stress. Take time out of each day to unwind mentally and to refresh yourself. What you do is up to you: for some, doing a crossword puzzle is a great escape from the pressures of the day; for others, reading several chapters from a novel, listening to music, taking a walk, or hitting a tennis ball may be an effective remedy. While some activities—playing golf, jogging, exercise—may also have desirable physical effects, their mental and emotional benefits are what we are seeking. What you do is not important; that you do *something* is important.

In a nightmarish daisy chain, pressure and stress cause one to worry, which leads to additional pressure and stress, which in turn cause more worry. We wish to recommend one method for reducing the amount of time you spend worrying each day. Designate 10 minutes of your day (preferably toward the end of the day) as your DWT—Designated Worrying Time. Look upon it as a "worry break." Anytime during the day that you begin to worry, stop yourself instantly and tell yourself that you must postpone all worrying until your DWT. "I will worry. I won't be cheated out of that," you may say to yourself, "but I must put it off until my DWT." At best, when your DWT arrives, you will have forgotten what you were supposed to remember to worry about; at worst, you will have limited dramatically the amount of time and psychic energy you spend each day in pressure- and stress-producing worry.

The Anxiety of Successful Women

One type of anxiety experienced in particular by some successful women is based on the conflict between what they were taught as children and what they are experiencing as adults in the workplace. In the 1950s and 1960s, they learned that "nice girls" should not be competitive, particularly with men. They were imbued with the notion that young women who were pushy or forward were exhibiting "masculine traits" and would be regarded as personae non gratae by men. Their role models were frequently women who stayed at home, raised families, and remained financially dependent upon their husbands for their entire adult lives. Of course some women did work outside the home during this period, but their jobs were not considered as significant or as prestigious as those of their male counterparts. Women as a group were simply considered less suited for successful careers than "the stronger of the species."

While certainly not every parent transmitted these notions to their children, many parents did. Furthermore, these attitudes extended beyond the home; young women, especially those raised in the 1950s and 1960s, could have easily confirmed these attitudes by simply looking about them.

Successful women, however, are living refutations of these antiquated ideas. Therein lies the problem. A successful woman's career, as well as the characteristics she acquires in the workplace, may place her in conflict with the values and truths taught to her by her parents and the environment in which she was raised. She may find that it is difficult to reject the values and truths acquired in her formative and most impressionable years without feeling a medley of emotions—regret, sorrow, embarrassment, anger, anxiety, and, in some cases, even guilt. Although she now accepts herself, her values, and her success on the intellectual level, there may still be the gnawing feeling that "I am not being a nice little girl."

Accepting Yourself in a New Role.   Probably the best antidotes for this problem are to understand the source of the negative feelings and to accept the fact that attitudes, social mores, and expectations are constantly changing, shifting, and evolving. Instead of being judgmental and thinking of attitudes, mores, and expectations as being right or wrong, think of them as having some appropriateness for the time period in which they occurred. The role of women, their role models, and their expectations have changed radically over the past 30 years. Relish the changes; enjoy the new horizons; delight in the richness of the workplace: Cheer the present instead of cursing the past.

A variation of the anxiety we discussed above occurs among women who believe that because they have become successful, they have, as a consequence, lost some of their femininity along the way. These women fear that success has meant sacrificing their female identity and acting more like men.

This myth falsely assumes that the behavior and personality traits of men define the only possible profile of a successful person. Even the most superficial observation of the workplace will give the lie to this assumption. One can readily see a plurality of profiles and observe numerous women who are both feminine and successful.

We also urge you to distinguish between substance and facade. Femininity is an inner quality, a quality of soul and spirit. It is not lost by wearing tailored suits and making tough decisions.

The Impostor Phenomenon

A large number of successful people feel uncomfortable with their success because they do not think that they have legitimately earned it. Instead of seeing their success as the result of hard work, dedication, tenacity, and high performance, they are convinced, as in the case of Susan S. from our last chapter, that their success is the result of "dumb luck," "being in the right place at the right time," "good fortune," or "the luck of the draw."

To make matters worse, they not only believe that they do not deserve their success, but they also live in fear of being exposed as frauds: "What if they find out that I'm really not *that good?*" "If I open my mouth, I know they will see through me"; "I don't think I could ever pull off that coup again."

These frightened individuals are totally convinced that sooner or later their colleagues and bosses and everyone else will discover that they are shams and impostors, that the truth will out and their houses of cards will come tumbling down. This type of problem has been ably described in a book called *The Impostor Phenomenon* by Dr. Pauline Rose Clance.[2]

"Impostors" are, in many cases, living paradoxes. They are successful but are convinced that they should not be or do not have a right to be. They work hard to be successful, but with each new success comes greater fear of being discovered. They want compliments on their work but are embarrassed at receiving them, not out of a sense of false modesty but because compliments make them feel guilty about their success. They want praise as a sign of affirmation, but it only increases their fear of exposure. They want to be successful but are sometimes afraid of taking the risks that accompany success for fear of failing. They want to enjoy success, but the more success they achieve the more intense are their feelings of guilt and fear. A sense of ever-present vulnerability—that something awful is about to happen—lives in every nook and cranny of their workplace lives. Enshrouded with feelings of guilt,

---

2. Pauline Rose Clance, *The Impostor Phenomenon* (Atlanta: Peachtree Publishers, 1985).

fear, deception, and hypocrisy, it is little wonder that they feel more like victims than successes.

One particular interesting result of feeling unworthy of success has been noted by Sheile Porter, a psychiatric social worker:

> Women who assume their job successes aren't the result of their own performance don't feel comfortable with the chief symbol of success, money. . . . I have clients who deliberately go on spending sprees or give gifts and money to others, simply to dispose of something they feel terribly guilty about having in the first place.[3]

You, Too, Have a Right to Be Successful and to Enjoy It. There are several steps that may be taken to overcome the impostor phenomenon:

• Accept the fact that you deserve to be successful. Better yet, demonstrate it to yourself. List all the achievements you have made during the past year. Now analyze precisely how they were realized, listing the elements that went into those successes: the time spend in researching an idea or project, the information you gleaned from colleagues and personal experience, the hypotheses that were created and then discarded, the late nights and weekends spent working on an assignment so that it would be completed on time, the hours spent rehearsing presentations, the sweaty palms while trying to land a big account, the butterflies in your stomach when you tackled a new project. In your orgy of unworthiness, you have forgotten the blood, sweat, and tears that went into your successes. *You* were their architect, not the fates or lady luck. Your successes were won the old-fashioned way, by earning them.

• Accept the fact that luck and timing do sometimes play a part in one's success. Rarely, however, are they the major or only ingredients in success. Luck and timing may sometimes give you a leg up, but it is through your hard work and talent that you manage

---

3. Quoted by Barbara Schecter, "Female Fears Hinder Path to Financial Success," *Columbus Dispatch*, 6 October 1987.

to get the other leg up and win the race. Furthermore, the work-place has an uncanny way of balancing good fortune with bad fortune; for every lucky break, expect a piece of bad luck as well.

• Accept the fact that you may have been given a break along the way—parents who paid for your education, a supportive spouse, or a good boss—but that is not what is primarily responsible for your success. Many people have been given the same or even better breaks and have not been successful. You were prepared to take advantage of what you were given and wise enough to make the most out of it.

• Accept imperfection in yourself. Everyone occasionally fails; it is not an indication that you are inadequate to the core. It is an indication that you are an active participant in the workplace and are human. Reflect on what happened to you and others when you did fail. Very little, we suspect.

• Apply your logic of failure to your successes. If you fail at a project, we suspect that you are all too ready to blame yourself. Apply the same logic to your successes: if you succeed, attribute it to yourself as well.

• Try to like yourself more and to believe in yourself. You are a decent, sincere, good person. People like you for yourself and not for your past achievements or promise of future successes.

Guilt and Family Life[4]

John F. was, by most standards, a successful executive. Naturally, this necessitated long hours at the office and work at home on weekends, but he was devoted to his family and always thought that he was spending sufficient time with them. His wife's protestations that he never seemed to have time for his family any more were summarily dismissed as gross exaggerations. When his youngest son's fourth-grade teacher called and asked if there was a problem at home that could account for the boy's rude behavior and poor grades, John F. was shocked. It was when he asked his son

---

4. See also our chapter "Working and Parenting" in *Transitions: Successful Strategies from Mid-Career to Retirement.*

what was wrong and the boy replied, "Daddy, you never have time to play catch anymore," that John realized that he was the problem.

"I made a mental list of all the activities I used to do with the family that had fallen by the wayside. The list was devastating—everything from shopping on Sundays to watching television to helping the kids with their homework. The change in how I allotted my time had occurred so gradually that I hadn't realized that I was neglecting the people who mean the most to me. I had acted from the best of motives, but I felt guilty as hell."

Success for many becomes a troubling achievement when they discover the negative, sometimes disastrous, impact it has had on the quality of their family lives. The time and energy and commitment it takes to become successful often leave little of those important commodities for one's family. The time you spend at home, which seems to grow increasingly brief, finds you in a physically fatigued, emotionally drained, and psychologically agitated condition. You are often too tired, too upset, too distracted, or too distraught to participate in family activities.

Furthermore, the pressures brought on by the workplace cause tempers to become short. Patience with spouse and children disappears; peccadillos become grievous faults; breezes become gales, tremors earthquakes, mists pea soupers. You are impossible to get along with, and you know it. Even the convenient rationale, "But I was working so that they could have a better life," offers little solace to either you or your family.

In a variation of this problem, some individuals we interviewed reluctantly expressed a sense of anger toward their children or spouses for interfering with their success. Some even confessed to wishing occasionally that they had never had children. These feelings are generally suppressed and often cause guilt, for they are seen as being socially and morally unacceptable, even unnatural. Parents become angry at the obstacles their children create and feel guilty for viewing their offspring as obstacles.

Resentment may also be felt by the children and spouse of a successful individual. They feel like unwelcome guests in that person's life. One woman complained, "Every time I want to talk to my husband at home, I feel like I am an employee asking for an appointment." Children and spouses become torn between the love they feel for the individual and the feeling that they are poachers trespassing on his or her work time.

It is little wonder that the successful individual will at times feel guilt and confusion over his or her success. This goal you have worked so hard to attain may have forced you to compromise the most important relationships in your life. The cost has been dear. Yet you cannot realistically divest yourself of success, for it has brought you and your family financial security, creature comforts, and a life-style you do not wish to abandon.

Winning on All Fronts.   Achieving success at the expense of your relationship with your family is a disturbingly costly achievement at best. We believe, however, that with planning and forethought you can have both a successful career and a warm and loving family relationship.

• Leave your work at the office, literally and figuratively. Try to avoid taking work home or receiving business calls at home; the time you spend at home should be devoted to your family and yourself. If you are thinking or worrying about work assignments, you may be physically present but you will be mentally light-years away.

• If your boss gives you an assignment that conflicts with a planned activity with your family, do a quick mental cost-benefit analysis of the short- and long-term consequences of each alternative. Do not be afraid to say "no" to your boss and to explain your rationale. He or she has probably been confronted with similar situations. If appropriate, you may try to arrange a more accommodating work schedule or a schedule that requires less work on weekends.

• Plan one or two special activities with your family each week. Going to dinner with your spouse or to a movie or the park with your children will let them continue to feel that they play a major role in your life. These activities should be scheduled in your calendar with the same care and commitment that you would schedule an appointment with your most valued customer. Furthermore, these activities often become the occasion for each party to discuss issues that are on his or her mind. One of our interviewees, Roger S., an academic whose specialty is program evaluation, asserted that the deepest and most honest conversations he ever had with his teenage children came during long drives he took with them to and from baseball and soccer games.

• Regardless of the difficulty it entails or the protests that it might occasion, we strongly recommend that you and your family eat the evening meal together. This is an excellent opportunity—often the only opportunity—for everyone to discuss the events, achievements, disappointments, problems, and successes of his or her day. It is a type of family staff meeting at which each person has the opportunity to update the other members of the family about what he or she has done and what he or she is planning to do; it is the time at which family members may experience the family as a unit.

• Explain to your family why your work takes so much time. A surprising number of people we talked to did not have a precise idea of what the family breadwinner did, much less how that individual spent his or her workday. Discuss with family members the unpredictable nature of any given day; the demands on your free time for entertaining clients; the degree to which your schedule is not under your control; spontaneous assignments; contingency plans; the responsibilities you feel toward your coworkers, boss, and firm; the precarious and uncertain nature of the workplace in general; and the pressures that a successful individual experiences. You may even want them to shadow you for a day at work. Providing them with a window into your working life may help them understand and accept workplace/family life conflicts and thus alleviate some of the guilt you are experiencing.

While we certainly do not wish you to minimize your obligation to your family, we do wish you to accept imperfection in your balancing act. Do not be alarmed if your family does not resemble the Cleavers of "Leave It to Beaver," or if you are not a combination of Dr. Spock, Mother Teresa, Donna Reed, and Job. Trying to be all things to all people is not humanly possible, and there is no need to feel guilty or angry about not being able to perform the impossible. Accept yourself as being a good parent and a good spouse and try to remember the words to the ancient prayer: "Lord, give me the strength to change what can be changed; the grace to accept what cannot be changed; and the wisdom to know the difference."

I Don't Have Time for Me

If you were to meet Jim C., you would be convinced that he had life by the tail. A successful entrepreneur, Jim had money, prestige, and job security. Yet he was miserable. "I feel like a distribution center giving away pieces of myself each day. I come to work an hour before everyone else as well as on Saturday mornings because once the doors open, everyone wants a part of me. I stopped going out for lunch because every time I returned there was a stack of yellow telephone slips on my desk. I give myself to my employees, to my clients, to my suppliers, and to the business until I have very little time and energy to give to myself. I get depressed when I think of it, but my employees probably have a richer life than I do. I don't even take vacations. I have time for everyone else, but I never seem to have time for me."

Jim C.'s lament is not uncommon among successful people, especially those who run their own businesses. People suffering from his problem will often ask basic questions about their lives: "Why am I working?" "Why am I earning money if I do not have the time to enjoy it?" "Is success simply a word, or is there a life-style that should go with it?" "Am I happy?" For many, the answers inspire feelings of resentment against their jobs and colleagues, and even anger at their success.

Time is an increasingly precious commodity. In the early years of a career, spending long hours at work may not have been troubling, for future time seemed limitless. When we reach middle age, however, it is natural to become protective of our time, to want to horde as much of it as we can, and to resent anyone or anything that steals it from us. It is little wonder that many people feel that their success has robbed them of what now has become so important: time.

Make Time. We hope the following recommendations will help you resolve the problem of time:

• In juggling the various demands on your time, be sure to leave time for the most important person—you, the juggler. If you are to avoid feeling exploited by your success, you must leave time for play, time to pursue activities that you enjoy, time to be alone, and time to do not one blessed thing.

• In determining what or who needs your time, all ties should be decided in your favor, when feasible. If you are unhappy, if you are displeased with yourself, or if you are stale, your work and those with whom you associate will soon feel the fallout.

• Schedule activities that you enjoy in the same manner and with the same determination that you schedule your most important workplace activities. You may wish, for instance, to play tennis one morning or golf one afternoon a week, or to set one evening aside each week for going to a movie, taking a class, shopping, seeing a friend, or coaching a children's athletic team.

• Whenever possible, leave your office for lunch; you need the break. Even if you cannot resist the obsession of constantly thinking about workplace issues, you will have at least changed your environment. This may help to distance yourself psychologically from your work.

• Maintain an active social life. This may take Herculean effort, but it is worth every ounce of it. There will always be innumerable valid reasons not to take the time to have dinner with friends, belong to social and recreational clubs, pursue hobbies, or take long weekends, but those reasons are not as important as maintaining your physical and emotional well-being. An evening with a friend, dinner with your spouse at a restaurant, or going to the theater will remind you of how pleasant a work-free, social evening can be.

• Finally, the most important recommendation: be good to yourself. You are the one person who should never feel short shrift.

The Success Is Not Mine

Mike S. is a successful lawyer. He is well known in his community, owns a home that looks like an English manor, and sits on several boards of directors. His is the profile of the successful professional, except for one problem: he hates his work. "I never made the decision to become a lawyer; I followed what my parents wanted for me. My father suffered through the depression and vowed that his son would have a profession. From the time I was in junior high, he keep telling me that I had to be a lawyer. By the time I discovered that I didn't like law, I was midway through law school. I thought it was too late to turn back; I had to pay back college loans, and life was moving too quickly. Besides, I couldn't tell my parents what I really wanted to do. I wanted to be a high school athletic coach. They would not have understood why someone would rather be a coach than a lawyer."

To indulge his interests, Mike S. takes every opportunity he can to coach his young sons' teams—soccer, baseball, basketball, and football—and is enormously successful at it, generally winning league titles. "I never get the highs in my work that I do coaching. I don't mind canceling appointments with clients if we need to have an extra practice. I would have been one helluva coach."

Mike S.'s experience suggests a fundamental truth that many successful people have discovered: Success is not personally satisfying if it is someone *else's* idea of success. Instead of deciding for themselves what they wish to do with their lives, numerous people uncritically—and at times unconsciously—follow the plans that others have for them. In one's formative and impressionable years, it is family and family friends that are likely to have the greatest impact on career decisions. As adults, it may be Madison Avenue that defines success as money, expensive cars, prestige, an opulent lifestyle. Individuals adopt these as valid indicators of success and look for a career that can grant them.

A variation of this problem occurs when some individuals find that while they may have originally selected an appropriate job or career, it no longer gives them a psychological high or feeling of fulfillment. A social worker, for instance, may no longer derive goal satisfaction from aiding a needy family; a real estate broker may fail to experience a rush of emotion and excitement after closing a deal.

Success Begins with You and in You. Your first allegiance in selecting a job or career should be to yourself. If your success is to bring you satisfaction and a sense of accomplishment and well-being, you must have a job or career that meets your expectations, values, and dreams, not the expectations, values, and dreams that others have for you. Shallow or meaningless victories provide little self-esteem or excitement.

If you discover that your specific job is not bringing you satisfaction, we do not suggest radical remedies, at least not initially. Rather, we recommend that you look for opportunities to perform the type of activities you do find satisfying while continuing in your present job. This may simply involve examining the diversity within your profession or firm and changing directions within the same field. If, for instance, despite your success in sales you still feel emotionally flat, you may wish to transfer to other offices within your firm, such as public relations or research and development, that you think you would find more fulfilling.

If you are like Mike S.—a fulfilling activity lies totally outside of your career or job—you may be able to pursue your interest in your spare time. We know of one university professor, for instance, who discovered in middle age that what really brought him satisfaction was acting. Not willing to give up a tenured position and a comfortable life-style, he simply spent all of his free time acting in local theater companies.

If you are deeply unhappy with your career or job and no relief can be found, we suggest that, despite your success, you seriously consider making a career or job change. Talk to friends and family about the problem, consult a career counselor if necessary, and make a painfully honest self-assessment. Work should be a source of fulfillment and self-realization, not a living nightmare.

SUCCESS AND FEELING GOOD

Although we have focused in this chapter on the problems of success rather than its joys, we wish to end on a positive note so that you will not curse your fate for being successful.

Success Signals Competence and Efficacy. Psychologists believe, as noted earlier, that feeling competent and efficacious are key ingredients to psychological health and contentment in the workplace. Your success suggests that you are a capable, resourceful, and effective individual. You are an initiator, a creator, and a problem solver; you are able to think analytically and logically, to perform skillfully and efficiently, and to lead forcefully and effectively.

We hope that you give yourself *time each day* to reflect on what you have accomplished, not in a boastful or vain fashion, but in an honest effort to acknowledge your achievements and how much you have grown and developed.

Success Signals Self-Awareness.   Success, as you have learned, does not come easily. Success means knowing how to live with failure, enduring temporary setbacks, making sacrifices, and coping with the vagaries of lady luck. Being able to deal successfully with the valleys as well as the peaks of the workplace suggests that you have attained a high level of emotional and intellectual maturity and self-knowledge. You have learned to manage your emotions and behavior, to deal with inner conflict and outer pressure, to understand your strengths and weaknesses, to become aware of your predilections and aversions; in short, you have gained insight into yourself.

Success Helps Others as Well as Yourself.   Success does not inhabit a void. It sends out ripples that touch many: your children, spouse, coworkers, and clients. Success creates options and opportunities for those around you, and in doing so it magnifies the good feeling your success initially brought you.

Success is Fun.   Achieving a worthwhile goal, setting your sights on an objective and attaining it, and giving form and substance to an idea are inherently enjoyable. It feels good to be a winner. We also wish to suggest that you savor the process of winning. In this way, the joy of final victory, which is sometimes brief, may be expanded to include the multiple successes that occurred along the way.

Success is elusive to some and unpleasant to others. Rarely is it easily achieved or fully enjoyed. We hope that our two chapters on the problems of success will help you understand its complex and demanding nature and its sometimes painful and poignant consequences. We want to help you to reach your potential, to stand to the full height of your capabilities, and to enjoy the view from the summit.

Chapter Six

Not All Prisons Have Bars

Overcoming Shyness, Vulnerability, and Intimidation

Mary S., a sales administrative coordinator for a large publishing house, rarely made eye contact with her colleagues when she spoke. When she walked her head was generally bent forward and her eyes were always focused downward, making her appear even shorter than her 5′ 2″. She started every conversation with an apologetic or self-effacing remark: "I am sorry to interrupt you," "I know how busy you are," "I know you probably don't have time to talk to me now."

Although Mary's work was superb—clear, timely, and always well thought through—she had difficulty using her skills to their full potential. Her boss was new to his job and needed all the help, advice, and counsel he could get, but Mary was too shy to offer her expertise. When the work of the office declined, Mary could never muster the courage to say what she needed from him to do a better job or how the office could function more productively or what was needed to put some fun back into the workplace. To do this one had to be assertive, and Mary was not that.

Phil S. began teaching as an assistant professor at a small college in California while he finished his dissertation at a nearby university. After teaching for one month, he felt fairly good about his performance in the classroom—that is, until he received a memo from his department chair one Monday morning requesting a meeting on Friday afternoon. When Phil nervously asked what the meeting was about, his chair said, "We'll talk about it Friday." Shy and diffident, Phil did not wish to push the matter any further; he knew he was in trouble. A student must have complained. Maybe his dissertation director had called the chair to say that Phil's dissertation was not of acceptable quality. Perhaps Phil had unwittingly done something unprofessional to a colleague. By Thursday, he was convinced that he was one day away from hearing the "F" word. When Friday finally arrived, he could barely stand without shaking. With his heart pounding, his mouth dry, and butterflies the size of Buicks in his stomach, he went into the chair's office, only to receive his first performance review, which, incidentally, was very positive. Phew!

Although both Mary and Phil are productive, talented people, they suffer from negative feelings or personality traits that will hamper their career progress and reduce their ability to enjoy their jobs. There are numerous adjectives that can be used to describe them: weak-willed, shy, vulnerable, intimidated, timid, reticent, bashful. We realize that these feelings and traits are not synonymous, but we believe that they are sufficiently related in their ability to influence and impact behavior in the workplace that they may be discussed collectively.

In this chapter, we wish to discuss the problems experienced by hundreds of thousands—perhaps millions—of workers who feel shy, vulnerable, or intimidated by bosses, colleagues, or the workplace in general and how to resolve those feelings.

KRYPTONITE AT WORK

There is nothing inherently wrong with being shy or bashful; there is nothing wrong with being aware of the pitfalls and land mines in the workplace; there is nothing wrong with being concerned about your welfare or your future at your job; there is nothing wrong with feeling defensive at times. It can be a jungle out there, and you should be cautious.

When, however, shyness, timidity, or feelings of vulnerability and intimidation prevent you from giving an appropriate representation of yourself—when they prevent you from expressing your feelings or ideas, when they interfere with your advancement or success in the workplace, when they block you from saying or doing what you wish, when they undermine your quality of life on the job, when they make you feel miserable—then those feelings and personality traits should be confronted and overcome.

Shyness, timidity, and feelings of vulnerability and intimidation may exact a high cost in the workplace. They often prevent their victims from getting a job, being promoted, achieving status among their peers, and reaching their full potential. How frequently, for instance, have we heard job interviewers rate applicants poorly because of their shyness: "Has little initiative." "I was looking for energy and found none." "Clearly lacks confidence."

Shyness, timidity, and feelings of vulnerability and intimidation may also cause painful inner conflicts. Behind an often placid exterior, their sufferers may desperately muse: "I wish I could stand up before a group and speak without feeling sick inside." "I am angry at myself for not explaining my ideas, but I just can't bring myself to do it." "Why am I always so afraid of authority figures?" "I wish I could feel more a part of things." Self-criticism at not being more assertive, confident, and positive is a common reaction. People can be disgusted at their own timidity.

How Careers Are Hurt

We wish to suggest several specific reasons why shyness, timidity, or feelings of vulnerability and intimidation may undermine one's career:

Lack of Interpersonal Skills. Communication skills are essential for advancement in the workplace. Being able to speak persuasively and clearly to clients, vendors, and customers; being able to speak forcefully and directly to subordinates; being able to speak cordially and openly with colleagues are vital to your career and personal welfare. In fact, with the increasing emphasis on people-to-people interaction not simply in sales but throughout the workplace, it is hard to imagine how one could survive, much less succeed, without having well-developed verbal and public presentational skills.

People who are inordinately shy or timid, however, or those who feel threatened or intimidated, often feel so awkward, nervous, and anxious when they have to speak that they avoid communicating whenever possible. And when they do communicate with clients, vendors, coworkers, and bosses, it is often done poorly. Furthermore, their shyness may inhibit them from asking pertinent questions, preventing them from acquiring information and stimulating the thinking of others. Since they try to avoid situations in which they will have to talk, attending staff, office, or company meetings becomes the equivalent of being placed on the medieval rack. At meetings they live in fear that they will be asked to speak or to respond to someone. We interviewed one shy individual who said he avoided being called on at meetings by continually looking down at his notes so that he would not make eye contact with anyone.

When shy, timid, or intimidated people do speak, they are often more preoccupied with their own embarrassment or uneasiness than with the clarity and forcefulness with which they express their points of view or ideas. They self-monitor their words and behavior so obsessively that they freeze themselves into human ice statues. Although they may have many wonderful ideas, those ideas are often inadequately and unpersuasively represented. They will often begin their remarks by saying, "I know this is totally wrong, but . . ." or "I know this sounds stupid, but . . ." or "You probably won't like this idea, but . . ." In fact, their aversion to public speaking can be so great that they are sometimes content to allow coworkers with whom they have spoken to express—even steal—their ideas and to take credit for them.

Isolation At Work.   Workers who are excessively shy or who feel vulnerable and intimidated often have difficulty relating socially or on a person-to-person basis with their coworkers. They may find it difficult to make friends or to develop cordial relationships.

Success at work, however, as we suggested in Chapter Four, often depends on being able to work closely and harmoniously with colleagues, to know that you can ask for their help and rely on their support. Completing large projects often demands professional networking: coalition building, seeking resources from other units, going beyond your office for personnel support.

A self-imposed isolation may also undermine an individual's contentment at work. Forming friendships, sharing time and interests, and interacting on a personal level with colleagues are among the most important reasons why people enjoy working.

Projecting a Negative Image. One of the unfortunate results of not communicating or relating optimally with colleagues is that they may misinterpret your isolation. Although shy or vulnerable individuals may in reality feel insecure, their coworkers may see them as proud, haughty, aloof, or snobbish. Job interviewers will sometimes describe them as "distant" or "not connecting." They may well become personae non gratae or social pariahs.

Excessively shy or vulnerable people will often hide their lights under proverbial bushels, compounding the problem. They may be very talented individuals, but they do not let others see the range and depth of their skills, abilities, talents, knowledge, and capabilities. They are not less intelligent or competent than their more assertive counterparts; it only appears that way.

Ultimately, the negative image that is projected to others may become a personal reality. If you believe that you will embarrass yourself by expressing an opinion, that people want to take advantage of you, or that you lack the self-confidence to take a stand, those beliefs may become realized. To an extent, you are what you believe. The shy or vulnerable or intimidated individual will look often upon himself or herself as inadequate, noncompetitive, and passive; as one who should not swing from the heels but be content with a base on balls or riding the bench; as one who should not try for victory but simply avoid defeat.

Furthermore, if you emit signals of vulnerability or intimidation, others may soon believe that you can be exploited or intimidated.

Your belief becomes their reality. We talked, for instance, to a secretary who was so cooperative and helpful that she could not refuse any work-related request of her boss. Whenever she was asked to work after hours, cover someone else's responsibilities, or handle a spur-of-the-moment request, she never refused. One evening she and her husband had planned a dinner party for twenty people. As luck would have it, a problem at work came up and her boss asked if she could stay late that evening. She immediately started thinking, "If my husband can get the appetizers in the oven, and if my sister can pick up the dessert, and if what I'm wearing now is dressy enough, and if my husband can entertain everyone for the first hour or so, I think I can stay at work." Her acquiescence and submissiveness were so well known that she allowed others to use and misuse her.

Adverse to Change.   Meeting new people, learning a new culture, confronting a new set of challenges, while hard for anyone, can be especially difficult for people who feel shy, vulnerable, and intimidated. Thus, they may be reluctant to change jobs, even if it is in their best career interest. As one such individual remarked, "A devil you know is better than a devil you don't know."

Changing jobs, however, is often an important strategy, even a necessity, for career advancement. One who wishes to be promoted must be willing to change jobs, relocate, and form new friendships—to put off the old and put on the new.

Self-Consciousness.   Shy, timid, and vulnerable people often feel overly self-conscious—the focus of all eyes—and sensitive to what others think of them. Thus, undertaking assignments and performing duties that most workers would take in stride may cause them consternation.

Their sensitivity to the impression they are making on others may cause them to feel criticism more deeply and acutely than their more outgoing colleagues. While evaluation of one's work may be anxiety producing for most people, it can be especially threatening to the shy or vulnerable individual. Moreover, even positive remarks about their work, such as "very good job" may be understood as "acceptable at best."

Misunderstanding a Boss and Colleagues. While they certainly do not have an exclusive claim to misinterpretation, shy, timid, and vulnerable people often misunderstand the words and behaviors of others. A boss's failure to say hello becomes a strong indication that he or she hates you; the laughter of colleagues gathered around the coffeemaker is probably at your expense; a mild criticism is a scathing diatribe about your work. Nor is a shy, timid, or vulnerable individual likely to have a sense of self-irony, which is important in maintaining one's emotional health on the job. These individuals are prone to making false assumptions, drawing fallacious conclusions, and, unfortunately, acting on those assumptions and conclusions.

Nonassertiveness. Shy or vulnerable people often do not trust their own judgments and as a result may tend to go along with someone else's idea even if they do not entirely agree with it. Since they want to avoid confrontations and disagreements they may avoid taking stands. When they do express an opinion, it is often in a tentative manner that fails to inspire confidence in others. In the presence of authority figures, their shyness, timidity, or vulnerability perhaps reaches its apogee. These feelings are likely to be exacerbated when they are asked to confer with their bosses, as in the case of Phil S., or to present reports to their supervisors.

Afraid of making mistakes or drawing attention to themselves, shy, timid, or vulnerable people will generally not be risk takers, will not try an approach or technique or project that may fail. By constantly monitoring themselves, by not wishing to think or act creatively or imaginatively, they place a limit on their potential achievements.

Avoiding Help. In a study of shyness, Peter Harris asserted that it is difficult for shy people to overcome their condition because they do not believe that others take their problem seriously.[1] They are afraid that colleagues, even medical practitioners, would simply

---

1. Peter Harris, "The Hidden Face of Shyness: A Message from the Shy for Researchers and Practitioners," *Human Relations* 37, no. 12 (1984), pp. 1079–95.

not understand what they experience or would not think that it is much of a problem.

We believe the same attitude is likely to be held by people who feel excessively vulnerable or intimidated. Their reluctance, even embarrassment, to seek assistance or to discuss their problem may inhibit them from receiving the counseling they desperately need.

THE INTERNAL SOURCES OF SHYNESS, VULNERABILITY, AND INTIMIDATION IN THE WORKPLACE

The causes of excessive shyness or feelings of vulnerability and intimidation often lie within the individual.

Fear of Being Emotionally Hurt.   Every time we offer an opinion, express an idea, or even start a conversation, we put our ego on the line. If our opinion or idea or attempt to start a conversation fails, we may feel uncomfortable emotions ranging from embarrassment to humiliation. Since no one likes to lose face or be laughed at or humiliated, we learn that discretion is the better part of valor. Rather than offering an opinion or idea, or reaching out to someone, we remain reticent.

As professors, we have too often seen students who have brilliant minds refuse to speak in class for fear of exposing themselves to criticism. There also seems to be a direct relationship between the size of the class and their reluctance to speak. While some may risk their egos before a group of 10 peers, very few are willing to hazard forward in a group of 100.

Burned in the Past.   The present is constantly being influenced by experiences from the past. If you have lost a job that you thought was secure, if you believe that you have received excessive criticism for acting decisively, if you have had your ideas rejected, if you have worked under a caustic boss, it is little wonder why you would now want to protect yourself.

When Jim L., a middle-level manager in a communications firm, began work he was an idealist. "If a firm is to progress, we must have a free and open exchange of ideas." His ideas, however, earned him the ill will of his boss, and he was soon fired. "My coworkers who never opened their mouths stayed on. I don't have to have a ton of bricks fall on my head to learn a lesson."

Poor Self-Image or Low Self-Confidence. Some individuals are shy or timid or feel vulnerable or intimidated because they feel that they have very little to offer. They are haunted by a negative, self-effacing inner voice: "Don't say that; you'll sound ridiculous." "Don't do that; it will place you in jeopardy." "Don't take on any extra responsibility. If you do, you could be held accountable." "Keep a low profile in order to protect yourself." Unfortunately, such individuals fail to understand that if they do not believe in themselves, no one else is likely to believe in them either.

Fear of Risk Taking. Since workers suffering from shyness, timidity, or feelings of vulnerability and intimidation are generally self-conscious and fear negative evaluations, it is less likely that they will wish to take risks. Doing the ordinary and expected, being flaming middle-of-the-roaders, playing their cards close to their vests, and backing into holes to protect their posteriors become infinitely preferable to sticking their necks out. A manager recently talked to us about a subordinate who, he said, "is driving me crazy." The subordinate was in charge of a small staff of three, but he was so frightened of making a mistake that he cleared everything—and we do mean *everything*—through our interviewee. The obsequious subordinate literally asked for permission to go to the bathroom. He also created a "forest and tree" problem: he spent so much time dotting "*i*'s" and crossing "*t*'s" that he would lose focus of the goals of his office. The manager described him as an "excessive micro-manager."

Inability to Separate Self From Work. If you fail to distinguish between yourself and your work, you will probably be profoundly and personally hurt if your work is criticized. If you feel that you—and not your idea or project—have been attacked or rejected, it will be unlikely that you will want to volunteer ideas or opinions or leadership in the future.

Reliving the Role of a Child.   Shyness, timidity, vulnerability, and intimidation may have begun at the hands and vocal cords of an overbearing or domineering parent. The sternness of parents and acerbic statements such as "don't speak until spoken to," "keep your opinions to yourself," "you are stupid," "can't you do anything right?" and "you are a disappointment" may reverberate for many years. Some shy, timid, or vulnerable workers may see their bosses as parental or authority figures.

Fear of Rejection by Peer Group.   People are sometimes shy, passive, and timid because they value group membership so much that they do not want to jeopardize their good standing in a group. Dr. Irving Janis of Yale University created the term "groupthink" to describe this phenomenon.[2] Groupthink occurs when people are so frightened of losing the warm, close, cohesive feelings of being members of a group that they self-censor any ideas that could cause them to lose their membership. They become "Yes People": Everyone agrees with everyone else, and no one plays the role of devil's advocate. Friendship at work and fulfilling social needs become more important than the quality of job performance.

The Need to be Loved Excessively.   Assertiveness, forcefulness, having the strength of your convictions, directness, and decisiveness can be invitations to conflict and altercation. Employees who need the emotional affirmation of others will want to avoid any words or actions that may alienate or estrange.

We knew of one manager who had such a great need to be liked by his subordinates that he would close his eyes to an array of outrageous abuses. Employees ruled the roost: they decided on how much work they should do and how long it should take. When some literally did not show up for work, the manager never confronted them. He succeeded in being well liked, but he was not respected. His desire to win the approval of his subordinates left him totally unable to represent the standards and expectations of the firm.

---

2. I.L. Janis, *Groupthink: Psychological Studies of Policy Decisions and Fiascoes,* 2nd ed., (Boston: Houghton-Mifflin, 1982).

HOW TO OVERCOME THE INTERNAL REASONS FOR SHYNESS, VULNERABILITY, AND INTIMIDATION IN THE WORKPLACE

Unlike the common cold, shyness, timidity, vulnerability, intimidation, and similar negative feelings are not conditions that will cure themselves. Overcoming them so that you can give an appropriate representation of yourself in the workplace demands effort and courage on your part. For many, the process is incremental and must be done in steps or stages. We believe the following specific suggestions may be helpful in your efforts to achieve your goal.

Mind Play.   Mentally act out in detail what it would be like to be more assertive, less timid, and less vulnerable. Picture yourself, for instance, walking into your boss's office and asking for a moment of her time. After sitting down in the chair facing her desk, calmly cross your legs and, while maintaining eye contact, announce the purpose of your visit: "I would like to talk with you about a raise."

If you have a presentation to make, playact in your mind the entire event. Picture where specific people generally sit, where you will stand, what you will wear, what your opening remarks will be, how you will respond to questions, the looks of approval from your audience, the good feeling of accomplishment you will experience when you are finished. If you can picture it in your mind, if you believe it can be done, then you are well on your way to accomplishing your objective.

The transition from thinking to acting can be very difficult; look for help in making this change. If there are coworkers, for instance, whose self-confidence and assertiveness you admire, use them as models to emulate. Ask yourself these questions:

• How do they speak?
• Do they use gestures when speaking?
• Do they look people in the eye when speaking?
• How would they react to a specific workplace problem or issue that I am facing?

- To what extent do I think they worry about keeping their jobs?
- Do I think they often feel victimized?

Role-Play and Rehearse. Take mind playing and observing role models one step further: role-play or rehearse with a friend, spouse, or trusted coworker an event that you will soon face. If you have an upcoming meeting, for instance, learn what the agenda will be and write out one or two questions that you wish to ask or a point that you wish to make. Practice your part much like an actor or actress would. At the meeting you may, in fact, feel like a performer about to go on stage, complete with sweaty palms and pounding heart. Role-playing and rehearsing, by the way, are not the exclusive province of the shy, vulnerable, or intimidated; confident, experienced, and forceful executives have also been known to employ them.

Make Changes Incrementally. Habits, behaviors, feelings, and personality traits that have developed over many years are not changed in a day or a week. Begin by making small changes in safe surroundings. Try asserting yourself, for instance, with a friend over where to eat dinner or what movie to see. Take a stand first on minor issues at work and then graduate to more significant matters. Set a goal to talk once or twice at a meeting, not to worry for an entire day about being fired, not to dread seeing your boss, or to talk to someone with whom you do not typically converse. Notice that people do not suddenly dislike you for being more assertive, nor have you lost your job. Often, in fact, your colleagues will have more respect for you. Life goes on, and generally for the better.

Stop Imagining a Catastrophic Future. Do not dwell on all the negative events that could take place: being fired, being embarrassed before your coworkers, being chewed out royally by your boss, losing a major account. Those events have probably not happened to you in the past, and there is no realistic reason to assume that they will occur in the future.

Think of a time in the past when you did make a mistake at work. Did you suffer any serious or long-term consequences? Did your life significantly change for the worse? Did anything of importance happen? The negative consequences are rarely as traumatic or dramatic as you may envision; catastrophes occur far more often in one's mind than in reality. Recognize your propensity for looking bleakly at the future and make a strong effort to overcome it. Better yet, instead of imagining disasters, envision your successes.

Avoid Being Overly Self-Conscious and Overly Self-Critical. People who are shy or timid or who feel vulnerable or intimidated are, as we described earlier, often overly self-conscious and self-critical. All eyes are not focused on you; you are not the center of the universe for your colleagues. In fact, it would probably be humbling to know how little others reflect on what you are doing.

Avoid taking sole responsibility if an interaction with a colleague fails. If a conversation, for instance, falls on its rhetorical face, remember that you are responsible for only 50 percent of the interaction. Perhaps the person to whom you spoke was abrupt, taciturn, or simply having a bad day. You are neither the center of the workplace nor the single cause of negative events.

Develop an Appropriately Assertive Style.   Practice speaking more forcefully and expressively. Use gestures when you speak; they are a valuable means for giving emphasis to your words and ideas. Hold your head high when entering a room; make eye contact when talking to a colleague; vary the pitch, volume, and tone of your voice; have the strength of your convictions.

If you wish additional help, join an assertiveness-training seminar, a support group, an organization such as Toastmasters, or enroll in a Dale Carnegie course.

Develop a Positive Self-Image.   Believe in yourself. If you feel good about yourself, if you believe you are a competent worker, if you have confidence in yourself, those positive feelings will come through to others. Take a few minutes each day to review all the "positives" that you have accomplished. You have worked hard and have a right to expect success in your career.

Recognize that Being Kind and Being Assertive Are Not Mutually Exclusive. Do not confuse a healthy representation of your thoughts, beliefs, opinions, and values with unkindness or rudeness. Self-representation does not mean being aggressive or belligerent. You can be assertive and strong yet still be diplomatic, professional, and cordial.

We observed a situation in which a manager in retailing needed a decision from his boss on whether he could make a job offer to a certain candidate. The manager's boss sat on the decision, thinking that the longer he waited the more he would maximize his options. Sometimes this strategy worked, but now it was hampering the effectiveness of the manager's office and the job performance of his subordinates.

The delay disturbed both the manager and the job candidate. The manager wrote an angry memo to his boss, but, fortunately, replaced it with a more diplomatic, objective statement of his needs. Phrases such as "you must respond" were replaced by "I would appreciate a decision because," followed by a reasoned argument rather than intemperate demands. The manager represented himself and his interests forcefully, yet without antagonizing his boss. He promptly received a positive decision.

Separate Yourself from Your Work. It is important to draw a distinction, as we said in Chapter One, between yourself and your work. You are a unique and worthwhile individual with hopes, dreams, goals, interests, and values; your work is what you *do* for a living. An idea or project is something that you produced; it does not define you as a person. Furthermore, there are numerous reasons why an idea is rejected or a project fails that have little to do with the quality of either.

Reward Yourself For Making Changes. Make a list of specific goals and reward yourself for achieving them. For instance, if you spoke at a meeting, made eye contact with a person you generally find intimidating, did not worry about your job security for a week, or disagreed with a colleague or your boss, reward yourself. The rewards can range from spending money on yourself to giving yourself a well-deserved pat on the back. Whatever the reward, make sure that it is something that has value and meaning for you.

Recognize that Your Negative Feelings Are Hurting Your Career and the Welfare of Your Firm. The workplace relishes doers, achievers, and decision makers (see "How to Achieve Success in the Workplace" in Chapter Four). Shyness, timidity, and feelings of vulnerability or intimidation may prevent you from becoming an active participant in the workplace. Furthermore, your reluctance to engage fully in the give-and-take of the workplace may adversely affect your firm. Your office and coworkers are not benefiting from your good ideas and experience; your talents, abilities, skills, and knowledge are not being fully utilized. Instead of being an active member of a team, you are content with being on the disabled list, denying to both yourself and your firm the advantage of the many contributions you could make.

THE EXTERNAL SOURCES OF SHYNESS, VULNERABILITY, AND INTIMIDATION

While the causes for excessive shyness, vulnerability, and intimidation often live within the individual, the workplace environment may also bring on or exacerbate these conditions.

Employees quaked in their boots when they saw him. They had good reason to, for he was the boss and to cross him, it was believed, was to put your job in jeopardy. No wonder turnover in the sales division was so high.

He had a way of verbally reducing healthy, well-adjusted individuals to emotional rubble. One technique was to treat them like children. On one occasion he saw an employee walk out of an elevator *before* a valued client. At 5 P.M., the livid boss asked the offending employee in a demeaning fashion, "Do you think you did anything wrong today? Can you think of anything that I might have seen?"

He was also a finger-pointer. And when he got mad, his voice boomed right through his protruding finger and lodged itself deep

within the employee's heart. Everyone walked on eggshells when he
was around.

The irony of the entire situation was that the boss was, underneath
a brusque exterior, a sweet, altruistic, and caring man. He had absolutely no idea of how he affected, intimidated, or impacted others.
Moreover, no one ever told him of how he was perceived. They were
too intimidated.

Intimidating Bosses and Coworkers.   The characteristics or behaviors of coworkers and bosses such as the one we just described
may cause you to react in a shy manner or to experience feelings
of vulnerability and intimidation. The rank, position, or age of an
individual—a boss, foreman, senior person, or authority figure—
may make him or her appear intimidating. At times an individual's
manner—a loud, booming, or barking voice, stern or severe facial
expressions such as a scowl or frown, physical gestures such as
folded arms, a forceful or aggressive persona—may cause you to
feel vulnerable or intimidated. A direct, brusque, or acerbic manner
of speaking may also cause you to withdraw.

Environments.   The environment or organizational climate of the
workplace may cause or at least exacerbate shyness or feelings of
vulnerability and intimidation. The opulent and austere-looking
furnishings in an "old-money" law firm, the frenetic pace of activity
at a brokerage office, the predominance of one gender in an office,
the cacophony and danger of a factory setting—each of these may
well cause a range of responses from mild discomfort to total fright,
from slight intimidation to complete retreat.

HOW TO OVERCOME THE EXTERNAL REASONS FOR SHYNESS, VULNERABILITY, AND INTIMIDATION IN THE WORKPLACE

Overcoming the external reasons for shyness and feelings of vulnerability and intimidation is your responsibility; it will not happen
unless you take steps to make it happen. We hope the following
recommendations will help you with the task.

Seek to Understand the Source. Some bosses, coworkers, or senior people appear to be brusque, aggressive, or intimidating, but in reality they may be teddy bears. At times the problem is in the eyes of the beholder. If you have a propensity to shyness or timidity, you may simply have a knee-jerk reaction to any authority figure, regardless of what he or she is really like.

Some bosses, coworkers, or senior people may affect an air of brusqueness, aggressiveness, or intimidation for various reasons. They may confuse, for instance, gruffness, curtness, or arrogance with leadership. They mistakenly assume that if they are kind to people or let their staff see what they are really like, subordinates will no longer respect them. Sometimes individuals who are very sensitive and tenderhearted will create an intimidating exterior to protect their feelings; their personae become a type of hard shell to shield them from the emotional dangers of the workplace. Occasionally, people who are themselves shy, vulnerable, and intimidated will try to create the opposite impression by wearing a mask of bravado and strength.

It is important in these and similar cases to separate appearance from reality, to look beyond or through the veneer or surface illusion that a person has established to the true nature that lies hidden beneath. By understanding better the individual you are working for or with, you may see that his or her personality should not have a negative effect on you.

Some bosses or coworkers may create an imperious bearing to mask their feelings of insecurity or inadequacy. We have been told about one manager, for instance, who was pompous toward his subordinates and highly critical of their ideas; nothing they did quite came up to his standards. The truth behind the facade, however, was that he had a poor track record in the company and knew it better than anyone.

Give Your Boss or Coworkers the Benefit of the Doubt. Most people, we believe, want to be respected and liked, *not* feared. Give bosses and coworkers the benefit of the doubt. Assume that they wish to work with you and not enslave you; that they want your goodwill, not your dread; that they want a handshake and not a genuflection; that they are not superhuman but are probably very much like you. The preconceived notions we hold when we encounter an individual have a way of becoming self-fulfilling prophesies.

Behavioral Shaping.   Behaviors that are learned can also become unlearned with the guidance of a patient teacher. You may be able to shape your boss's behavior. If, for instance, you would like your boss to express appreciation more openly toward your work or to act more courteously toward you, you may wish to show your pleasure with a smile or a compliment when he or she nods positively: "I appreciate your support." As your boss begins to move in the behavioral direction you wish, continue to reward him or her by saying, "I enjoyed talking with you" or "It is wonderful to see everyone pulling together on a project" or "It is a pleasure to work in an office with such an esprit de corps." Your positive responses should help to reinforce the desired behavior.

Assert Yourself.   We spoke earlier about the importance of developing an assertive style for overcoming the internal causes of shyness, vulnerability, and intimidation. A sense of firmness, assertiveness, vigor, and determination will also help you interact successfully with intimidating people. When your voice is firm, your shoulders are held back, your head is high, and you believe in what you are saying, others may appear less frightening to you. They may even perceive you differently and behave in a less intimidating fashion in the future.

Be Diplomatically Honest.   Honesty is often the best policy. Consider broaching with your boss, in a thoroughly diplomatic, polite, and professional manner, the issue of your feelings of timidity. If you have a propensity toward shyness and vulnerability and you believe that you will benefit from revealing this to your boss, you may wish to explain that some of his or her remarks have exacerbated this condition. Encourage your boss to see that disagreement with his or her directives or methods is not the beginning of a coup d'etat but may, in fact, be healthy and productive. Explain that the morale, effectiveness, and productivity of your unit will be enhanced by creating an atmosphere of openness and amiability rather than fostering an intimidated silence.

One caveat: Evaluate your audience. Some bosses, no matter how diplomatically you speak to them, will blink at the clear light of truth. Weigh the costs and benefits of approaching your boss before acting.

Buy Time. At the precise moment you are in the throes of being verbally intimidated or put down, it is often difficult to respond effectively. Give yourself sufficient time to collect your thoughts and to respond with equanimity and coolness. This may entail physically leaving the area. If the abuse or intimidation is taking place over the phone, tell the speaker that you have some pressing business to attend to and will call back later. Doing so takes the initiative away from the intimidator while allowing you to formulate a response and self-manage your feelings.

If your boss is asking for legitimate information or making a reasonable criticism but you find his or her manner intimidating, you may be best served by buying time rather than blurting out a flustered or inarticulate response. A remark such as, "You're asking a good question. Can I come back in an hour and give you a more detailed and thoughtful response?" will allow you to represent yourself properly.

Respond to Intimidating Behaviors. It is generally emotionally healthier and in your best interest to respond resolutely to intimidating behaviors. If you are bothered, for instance, by a colleague's litany of how easy it is to be fired or of war stories about past employees, or if you are annoyed at having someone sit on the corner of your desk or stand too close to you when talking, stop the offending behavior immediately. Suffering in silence will only insure that nothing will change. Moreover, you may become angry with yourself for remaining passive.

Humor may also be invoked in a diplomatic way to send a message: "Sometimes I think if you were to stand any closer to me, you would be behind me."

Take the High Road.   In responding to intimidating or bullying behavior, maintain your dignity and pride. Backbiting or sarcasm offer only momentary relief and are unworthy of you. One effective way of dealing with intimidators is to turn their behaviors into offers of assistance: "You seem unhappy with my idea. How can I move the discussion in a direction that you would find useful?" "I am interested in the welfare of this office. What can I do to help?" "If you don't like my presentation, would you let me know the specifics so that I can improve it before I see our client?" "You seem angry. What can I do to help?" Such questions may prove disarming, while allowing you to present yourself as a conscientious employee.

Develop a Support System.   Share your problem with a friend, family member, or trusted coworker. Simply describing offensive people that you have encountered and receiving reassurance should make you feel somewhat better. Besides offering you advice on how to handle difficult people, your support system should remind you that most of the people in your life are amiable and kind.

If You Cannot Work with Your Boss or Colleagues, Consider Leaving Your Job.   If you have a boss or colleagues who make you feel so vulnerable, intimidated, or threatened that your work and the quality of your life are adversely affected, a job change may be advisable. When interviewing for a new job, be especially attentive to the personal characteristics of the person for whom you will be working and, if possible, your future coworkers.

Before you leave your job, however, try to determine if your boss or colleagues created the problem or if the problem was self-induced. If the problem lies within you, changing jobs will probably solve little. If you have tried the solutions for overcoming internal feelings of shyness, vulnerability, and intimidation that we have suggested but to no avail, you may wish to take the next step and seek professional counseling.

AND THE WINNER IS . . .

Unlike some of the problems we have discussed in earlier chapters, shyness and feelings of vulnerability and intimidation arise not so much from the workplace as they do from deep within the individual. They do not admit of a quick fix; rather, it takes courage, hard work, and enormous persistence to overcome them. Even marginal changes, however, in the direction of assertiveness, self-representation, and confidence are significant. This chapter will be in your corner as you spar with feelings of shyness, vulnerability, and intimidation. We hope that even if you cannot quickly administer a knock-out punch, simply engaging them will help you to feel better about yourself and your job.

Chapter Seven

"Go Ahead, Make My Day"

Anger in the Workplace

Most quarrels are inevitable at the time; incredible afterwards.

—E. M. Forster

P opping the cork, unfortunately, does not always refer to opening a bottle of champagne. The phrase describes perhaps the most destructive, debilitating, disruptive, and disturbing (we like alliteration) emotion in the workplace: anger. Our colloquialisms for anger—"blowing my stack," "blasting off," "boiling over," "making my blood boil," "driving me mad," "lashing out," "up in arms," "a seething cauldron inside," "having a short fuse," "flipping my lid"—suggest the violence and agitation that it inspires.

It should not be surprising that people experience and express angry feelings at work. In a broad cultural sense, it may be in part a result of our American tradition of rugged individualism. We have come to believe in the Horatio Alger, John Wayne, Rocky, and Rambo myths: all things are possible; the human spirit is capable of reaching any heights and achieving any goal; and if someone or something stands in our way, we will quickly remove the obstacle.

Thus, when we confront a boss who does not seem to be supportive, a client who is not cooperating with our desires to reach new sales records, a colleague who does not understand our goals, or traffic that keeps us from keeping an important meeting, we want to blow the offending parties away and bulldoze through the cars in front of us. Those uncooperative louts and cars are inhibiting us from achieving the success that is our manifest destiny, the success that we know we could achieve if only these impediments could be removed—at least according to the myths.

In a less cosmic context, the workplace itself is inherently fertile ground for anger. Numerous talented, ambitious, high-spirited people are working, often intensely, in close quarters for eight hours a day. As the pressures of work increase, it does not seem difficult to predict that toes will be stepped on, fingers will be burned, nerves will be frayed, tempers will grow short.

Furthermore, even though an office may have an overriding mission that encourages an esprit de corps and spirit of cooperation, each individual is also working on his or her own agenda. Each individual is working toward future goals and objectives in the firm—promotions, recognitions, awards, bonuses, perks. Each individual is on his or her own timetable for success. Add to the inherent competitiveness of the workplace the fact that each individual also has a private life that may occasionally fail to resemble paradise, and we are left with a volatile mix of ambition, egocentricity, aspirations, passion, personal problems, and emotional hurt.

There are also anxieties and frustrations within us that may cause angry outbursts. Each of us has an idealized view of what we are like as an employee, of how relationships at work should function, of how the workplace itself should be. We soon realize, however, that this idealized view generally does not conform to what is. Where we wish excellence in ourselves, we may find only adequacy; where we wish honesty in relationships, we may find duplicity; where we wish order and fairness in the workplace, we may find confusion and bias. The anxieties and frustrations caused by the disparity between our desires and expectations and the realities of ourselves and the workplace may be the source of angry eruptions at colleagues, clients, bosses, machines, events, and, most important of all, ourselves.

There are, of course, many causes for anger in addition to the ones we have suggested, but given the myths we live by, the competitive conditions of the workplace, and the disparity between desires and reality, we are not surprised at the amount of anger that is expressed at work.

THE BEASTS OF ANGER[1]

The Raging Bull: Aggressive Anger

While anger has numerous shapes and forms, blind rage or unadulterated wrath is probably its most obvious (and ugliest) manifestation. Often this type of anger is immediate, aggressive, out of all proportion to the stimulus, and induces behaviors that may border on the irrational. The raging bull impulsively lashes out at hapless victims, ignoring the canons of civilized conduct and oblivious to thoughts of future consequences. If no one is nearby, this bullying animal will vent his or her anger on inanimate objects: pencils become splinters, waste cans turn into scrap metal, and entire desks are cleared in one sweeping gesture. Predictably, this type of anger often leads to self-defeating words and deeds and eventual embarrassment.

The following letter, sent to Stephen Strasser's syndicated newspaper column "Working It Out," suggests some of the characteristics and consequences of this type of behavior:[2]

Dear Working It Out:
My ex-boss was a delight to work for—until I corrected a grammatical mistake of his. Then he became an ogre.

I felt very good about my new job. After working as a secretary for a short time, my boss gave me a terrific performance review. He said

---

1. Several of these concepts also appeared in *Working It Out: Sanity and Success In the Workplace.*

2. Stephen Strasser and Tom Bateman, *Working It Out.* Syndicated column with King Features.© Stephen Strasser, 1987.

he was very pleased with my work and recommended a nice salary increase.

I especially appreciated the compliments because my boss had let me know that he had been a straight-A student in college and considered himself a perfectionist.

Less than a week later, while typing a document for my boss, I noticed an error in punctuation. So, I checked a reference book. When I turned in the material, I jokingly said, "I punctuated the sentence the way the reference book suggested rather than the way you did." My boss turned purple with rage. He was furious.

The next day the office manager came up to tell me that I was being let go since my work was not up to par. I was stunned. I asked her why I had just received rave reviews and a raise if I was not doing a good job. She showed me an entirely different performance review which gave me poor marks for almost everything. Evidently my *other* evaluation had not yet gone through the necessary channels.

What do you think?

Miffed

The boss's actions suggest some of the costs of impulsive and oppressive anger: he and his office lost the services of a talented secretary, and "Miffed" lost a job. While we shall discuss methods for managing the expression of anger later in this chapter, we wish to describe briefly several basic mistakes made by the boss in dealing with his anger:

1. *Shooting from the hip.* Instead of thinking about the seriousness of the event—correcting a grammatical mistake—for a few hours or even sleeping on it, he chose to react immediately. Instead of allowing his emotions to subside and his slightly bruised ego to recover, he selected to hastily vent his spleen.

2. *I can't take it any longer.* In the give-and-take of the workplace, correcting a grammatical mistake does not seem to be the stuff of great tragedy. His reaction was vastly out of proportion to its stimulus.

3. *Keep it in focus.* Instead of dealing with the specific event that triggered his anger and directing his reaction to it, he chose to generalize his anger to include the entire workplace performance of his secretary. What should have been, at best, a local issue became a global issue with a draconian solution. If he had focused

on the event itself, we believe he may have seen that firing his secretary was a gross overreaction.

4. *Me Tarzan.* One of the most abusive displays of anger occurs when it is directed by a boss toward a relatively defenseless subordinate. The boss could selfishly indulge himself in his anger because he knew that his secretary could not respond. He used his rank not to foster the professional growth and development of a subordinate and the general welfare of the office but to punish and injure.

5. *Not Knowing Oneself.* The key to the boss's reaction may lie in his secretary's description of him as a perfectionist. Perfectionists often have difficulty accepting imperfections, even minor ones, in themselves. It would appear that his reaction was not to the behavior of his secretary as much as it was to his perception of a weakness in himself.

His remark to his secretary that he had been a straight-A student in college also suggests an element of insecurity. Secure people generally do not have to announce their brilliance. If the boss had been more introspective, if he had better understood his own weaknesses and sensitivities, his reaction may have been less extreme.

6. *Assuming the Worst.* Instead of assuming that his secretary respected him and was trying to do no more than simply correct a mistake, the boss assumed the worst. There is no reason to assume that his secretary was trying to hurt or humiliate him or to arouse his anger; there is every reason to assume that she wanted to get along with him.

7. *Killing his options.* If the boss had wished to respond to the secretary's correction, or if he had felt that the secretary was acting presumptuously, there were numerous options open to him. He could have joked back at her ("None of our clients is that literate"); accepted the correction, however reluctantly; averred (correctly) that grammar books generally lag behind trends in daily usage of language; or simply insisted that the mistake remain uncorrected. Any of these reactions would have kept the event circumscribed. His rage and the subsequent firing, however, precluded alternative and mutually beneficial courses of action.

8. *Nothing has changed.* If the boss thinks that he has removed the cause of his anger, he is deluding himself. The real cause of his anger lies somewhere else. It may be rooted in his feelings about himself, it may be the result of his relationship with his boss, or it may be a personal problem that is gnawing at him. Since he has not addressed the source of his anger, nothing has changed. It is highly likely that his former secretary will not be the last victim to feel his wrath.

Shooting Yourself in the Foot.   Ultimately, the boss's consumptive anger and pulsing rage benefited no one and hurt everyone. The secretary suffered the financial and psychological impact of losing her job. If she has a family, the deleterious effects may ripple out further, affecting the welfare of her children. In addition, although it may not be true in this particular case, employees who feel that they have been mistreated by a boss against whom they cannot retaliate will sometimes retaliate against those closest to them—their children, spouses, and friends.

The boss lost a valuable employee, one who was providing the office with "terrific performance." It is entirely conceivable that her departure may adversely affect the productivity of the office. Furthermore, finding excellent secretarial help, like solving most staffing problem, is difficult as well as expensive. A fairly recent study reported that it costs an average of $7,700 to replace a secretary.[3]

Finally, the boss has ultimately hurt himself. If the productivity of his office declines, his reputation will suffer. If other subordinates see that their boss is capable of capriciously firing an employee, their morale, loyalty, and productivity may deteriorate. His actions have not created the healthy and supportive atmosphere in which employees flourish. Furthermore, the boss, if he reflects with candor on the firing, may have difficulty accepting what he has done. His moment of glory may cause him longer-term feelings of guilt.

In general, the raging bull only succeeds in frightening people and driving them away. If you respond with consumptive anger

---

3. Allen Fishman, "Business Insight," *Columbus Dispatch*, 11 January 1987.

at losing an important account, failing to get a well-deserved raise, or being fired, you will turn people off at the very time when you need them the most. This type of anger isolates and separates; it prevents those around you from providing the emotional support and sympathetic balm that would alleviate some of the distress.

The Sly Mouse: Passive Aggression

Anger may also be expressed in a subtle, indirect, or behind-the-back manner. If, for instance, the secretary above had kept her job but remained piqued at her boss for his temper tantrum, she may have "inadvertently" forgotten to type an important letter, "unintentionally" misfiled a vital document, or "accidentally" forgotten to give her boss an urgent message. These passive-aggressive behaviors may be done in a fully conscious, premeditated effort to retaliate for a boss's anger, or they may be unconsciously performed. In either event, the effect on the boss or manager may be devastating.

The *Diagnostic and Statistical Manual of Mental Disorders* (DSM-III) provides a useful illustrative definition of passive aggression:

> Individuals with this disorder habitually resent and oppose demands to increase or maintain a given level of functioning. This occurs *most clearly in work situations*, but is also evident in social functioning.
>
> The resistance is expressed indirectly, through such maneuvers as procrastination, dawdling, stubbornness, intentional inefficiency, and "forgetfulness." For example, when an executive gives a subordinate some material to review for a meeting the next morning, rather than complain that he or she has no time to do the work, the subordinate may misplace or misfile the material and thus attain his or her goal by passively resisting the demand on him or her. Similarly, when an individual always comes late to appointments, promises to help make arrangements for particular events but never does, and keeps "forgetting" to bring important documents to club meetings, he or she is passively resisting demands made on him or her by others.[4]

---

4. *Diagnostic and Statistical Manual of Mental Disorders*, 3rd ed. (Washington, D.C.: American Psychiatric Association, 1980), p. 328. DSM III-R is currently available. Emphasis added.

Not only is the boss or manager adversely affected by the passive aggression of an employee; the subordinate is also. The individual appears to be inefficient, careless, or apathetic and may thus be passed over for promotions, merit raises, or better assignments. The expression of anger is rarely a simple matter; the anger of one individual toward another may damage the careers and emotional welfare of both.

The Bosom Serpent: Suppressed Rage

We take the name for this type of anger from an ancient folklore motif. In the traditional narrative, a person ingests a snake ovum that grows and develops within his or her bosom. The snake continually feeds and gnaws on the individual, causing physical and emotional pain and illness. The only cure is to expel the reptile; failure to do so will result in the further consumption and eventual death of the person.

Several years ago we were told about the travails of John J., a highly successful investment banker in New York City. His career allowed him to have many of the trappings of wealth and privilege: a home in an exclusive suburb, his own tennis court and swimming pool, and membership in a prestigious golf club. While John projected to the world an image of satisfaction, confidence, and fulfillment, a savage war raged inside of him. He had a boss who was jealous of his talent, the image he projected, his silver-spoon background, the schools he attended, and the life-style he enjoyed. His boss was relentless in his criticism and took every opportunity to disparage John's accomplishments to others. John thought that the best course of action was to avoid talking to his boss as much as was feasible. Silence, however, did not quell the overwhelming rage John felt inside. Not wishing to burden his wife and children with this problem, and afraid of talking about it with colleagues, he kept his serpent caged deep within himself.

Added to his silent and suppressed anger was a great deal of anxiety created by the unforgiving nature of his institutional clients. He worried that his home and life-style were largely functions of economic trends and world markets over which he had no control.

The physical manifestations of John's inner anger—gastrointestinal problems and headaches—were ignored until he started to lose his hair, not by the strand, but by the clump. That was the final shock. He sought professional help to deal with his suppressed rage.

The serpent in the bosom may also arise from our failures and foibles, for not achieving what we think we should achieve. If, for instance, you make a presentation at a meeting and a colleague calls your entire report into question because your data are not the most current, you may become privately angry at yourself. "She was right," you muse, "I should have checked my data. I hate myself for being so stupid." For the rest of the day your stomach muscles remain tightly contracted.

While the raging bull may terrify and savage anyone unfortunate enough to be within earshot, those who suppress their anger allow the serpent to gnaw at their stomachs and poison their spirits. Suppressed or unexpressed anger may feed on the individual, grow at his or her expense, and, like Frankenstein's monster, threaten to destroy its creator.

The Omnivorous Shark: Misdirected Anger

Some anger is displaced, misdirected at someone other than the person who inflicted the hurt. Like a shark, the person who experiences it may attack virtually any moving target, indiscriminately showing his or her ferocity. An individual may be angry at a boss or at himself or herself, but instead of confronting the true source of the anger chooses to assail an innocent bystander. Often the victim is a subordinate who cannot fight back directly.

Indiscriminately attacking relatively safe targets may, of course, cause them to respond with passive aggression. One manager we know would get so angry—cheeks flushed, eyes flashing fire—that after verbally excoriating the person who caused the anger he would, like the omnivorous shark, troll for anyone else he could find. "By God, none of them is carrying his load!" His subordinates responded by doing the absolute minimum that was required. Eventually, some of them turned their passive aggression into positive action: they quit.

This type of displaced anger is frequently allied with scape-goating. For instance, an executive who loses an account may blame his innocent secretary for not finding the correct information from a file or for not mailing letters earlier. Scapegoating may also take the form of racial, ethnic, or gender prejudice. The individual who applies for a job and is not hired may, for instance, denounce minority groups for allegedly having some type of advantage: "If my skin had been a different color, I would have been hired. The firm needed more minorities on the payroll." A sales manager whose staff is underperforming may realize that he has failed to motivate them but find it easier to direct his anger at others: "If we didn't have so many women working here, our bottom line would be better. They don't know how to be aggressive."

SLAYING THE BEASTS

Since anger can be such a debilitating and destructive emotion at work—disrupting the productivity and tranquility of the individual experiencing it and many of those around him or her—it is vital that we learn methods for dealing with this emotion.

"Yes, I Am Angry."   Before an emotion or behavior can be managed, it must first be acknowledged. Some individuals refuse to admit to their anger because they believe any of a number of misconceptions: "nice" people do not get angry, people will not like you if you get angry, all anger is bad, expressing anger at work in always unprofessional, good people are always in control of themselves.

Since few of us are candidates for canonization, you should not feel guilty if you experience the emotion of anger; you will not suddenly grow pointed ears and a tail. Anger is, to paraphrase Eldridge Cleaver, as American as apple pie. The problem is not so much in experiencing the emotion but rather in how you express or deal with the emotion. Anger may even, as we shall see, be a positive emotion, prompting us to work better and smarter.

Sharpening Your Sword: Identify the Source of Your Anger.   If the beasts of anger are to be slain, their sources—the remarks, issue, events, or people that gave them life—must be clearly identified and often confronted. Determine the present cause of your anger. You may, for instance, assert that a certain individual elicits your anger, when in reality it is not the individual but something that he or she specifically says or does. If you discuss your feelings of anger with him or her, you are more likely to reach a reasonable solution if you address what specifically offends you than if you sound as though you wish to declare the individual anathema.

If an event or issue arouses your anger, identify—as you did with the offending individual—the specific element that starts your blood racing. If, for instance, you become angry because a colleague is promoted ahead of you, try to determine precisely what it is that bothers you. Is it a sense of injustice that an undeserving person was promoted? Is it the poor judgment or lack of discrimination of the boss? Is it recognition that your inherent shyness or reticence stood in your way of asking for a promotion? Is it what you perceive to be office politics? Is it pure and simple jealousy of him or her?

Identifying sources of anger correctly and clearly is not always a simple task. You may, for instance, avoid looking at your own behavior as a contributing factor to your anger, or you may avoid identifying a person who evaluates your work. Time, honesty, introspection, and reality testing are critical ingredients to an accurate diagnosis.

Sticks and Stones Can Break My Bones, but Words . . . Confront the Source.   There is disagreement among psychologists about how freely we should vent our anger. To some, the "let it all hang out" school of thought, we should immediately express our anger totally and without reservation. To others, such as Carol Tavris, we should try to stake out a middle ground: "what's called for today is not the ungoverned gush of raw feelings, but a new civility that accommodates the expression of angry emotions."[5]

We agree with this centrist position. Expressing anger over everything that bothers or annoys us would lead to a very uncivilized—

---

5. Carol Tavris, *Anger: The Misunderstood Emotion* (New York: Simon & Schuster, 1983).

to say nothing of noisy—workplace. Anger would be the modus operandi instead of the exception to the rule. Of paramount importance, we believe, is not only learning to express our feelings in an appropriate manner but also determining how to deal with the causes of the anger.

If you feel anger to the point that it is troubling or irritating you, go to the source of the problem, if possible. Verbalize what is specifically bothering you. Tell the object or source of your anger, as calmly and as honestly as you can, that you *are* angry and *why* you are experiencing this emotion: "I am uncomfortable with the way you address me." "I need more help from you in getting this project done." "I'm concerned about the equity of my pay." Suggest the possible effects of this inappropriate behavior: "It will be very hard to work well with you unless I feel that I am respected." "It won't be fair to the others to include your name in the report unless you write your section." "The inequity in my salary is affecting my morale."

Finally, show concern by offering potentially corrective measures: "Why don't you just refer to me by my first name?" "What can I do to help bring you on board on this project?" "Can you tell me what I must do to warrant a raise?"

In your discussion with the individual, be sure to remember that you are not trying to intimidate or threaten but rather to explain and resolve. Name calling, an acrimonious tone, or vindictiveness are inappropriate as well as counterproductive; they will only incite more anger in yourself and the person you are addressing.

This reasoned, composed exchange should take place soon, if not immediately, after you begin to feel angry. The longer you wait, the more exaggerated and distorted the issues often become. Molehills grow into proverbial mountains; breezes become hurricanes; showers become deluges.

At times you will discover that simply expressing your feelings and their rationales may make you feel better. Equally important, this honest exchange may serve as the basis for a reconciliation or at least a clearing of the air.

One caveat: Some people may resent discussing these issues, even in a nonthreatening manner. If you believe this is the case, rely on your support systems and other outlets for alleviating your negative feelings.

Stay On Target. When you talk to the individual responsible for your anger, keep your focus specifically on the offending issue. Describe the specific reasons why you are displeased. Do not allow issues from prior altercations or extraneous matters to muddy the waters. Above all, do not make an ad hominem attack by bringing into the discussion the private life or personality of the individual (unless, of course, personality is the issue).

Think beforehand of what you are going to say, and do not overstate your position: "You could force a Dale Carnegie instructor to punch you out." "You could make the entire female gender celibate." Doing so will only cause your remarks to lose their credibility. The recipient will think that you are making a personal attack rather than initiating an intelligent, objective discussion of differences in an attempt to resolve a conflict. Furthermore, overkill will probably provoke an overresponse to your remarks, with the anger escalating on both sides. Make your case reasonably and politely; the rest is up to the recipient.

Talk Behind Closed Doors. Hold your discussion in private and allow adequate time. Confronting an individual in a public setting will probably embarrass him or her, provide weeks of grist for the office gossip mill, and make resolution of the problem more difficult.

Be Politely Assertive. If a calm, nonthreatening discussion is not productive, do not be afraid to be politely assertive. Assertiveness is preferable to anger. Instead of suffering in silence, have the strength to say, "I don't like what you just did." "I thought you were wrong at the time, and I still do." "I do not wish this to happen a second time." If you are assertive without showing your fangs or flaring your nostrils, and if you express measured, not hysterical, emotion, your words may lead to some type of resolution of the problem.

Have Realistic Expectations. Do not expect a road-to-Damascus experience in which the offending party will make a sudden and miraculous change immediately after hearing your words. Behaviors and attitudes are not easily altered, but you have made a start. Your words may not immediately bear the fruits you desire, but give them a chance to germinate, take root, and help the individual to grow.

Game Plans: Anticipate And Prepare. Anticipate and prepare for encounters that are likely to produce anger. If, for instance, you feel strongly that you deserve a raise but are uncertain how the boss will react to your request, rehearse what you will say and do if you get a negative response. If you wish to avoid an angry and emotional outburst, which will do little to prove to the boss that she made a bad decision, have a good idea of how you will respond to bad news.

You may wish simply to disengage: "Thank you for your time." "I'm glad I had a chance to express my thoughts and feelings about this matter." You may wish to ask for the promotion policy in your department or for the boss's specific rationale for denying you a raise, and to respond later: "Let me think about what you have said and get back to you in a few days." "Give me a chance to consider your reasons and I'll respond in a memo." These measured responses will suggest your maturity and professionalism, perhaps produce answers to your questions, and will certainly increase your chances of leaving your relationship and lines of communication with your boss intact.

Call Time Out. If an unexpected event occurs—if, for instance, your boss or a colleague criticizes your work unfairly and you are genuinely taken off guard and flustered—take control of yourself and the situation by disengaging. "Let me get back to you about that" or "Let's talk about that privately" or "I am in the middle of something now but wish to pursue that point with you" will allow you time to cool your emotions, analyze precisely what was said and meant, and devise a strategy for answering the person.

Can You Top This? Humor is generally a socially acceptable way to make a strong point or to be pleasantly assertive. Whether to use humor to express your anger and to confront the specific behavior you dislike is, we think, largely a matter of personal preference. Some people find it difficult to direct a joke at someone, while others seem ready to step into David Letterman's shoes. One way, for instance, of dealing with the office oinker is with wit that he would understand: "I don't like your sexist behavior, and I find your sexist jokes to be demeaning to women. I know this may astound you, but most women would not take it as a compliment to be told that they look like they could nurse a developing country."

Know Thyself. You may wish to keep an Anger Log of when you feel angry. Any time you are moved to anger, record the event, the time, the offending remark, the situation, and the person who caused you to react. By reviewing such a log, you may be able to learn more about your sensitivities, the types of words or issues to which you react, and patterns in your behavior. If, for instance, you discover that there are certain events or specific individuals that generally provoke your anger, you should try to avoid them if possible. If avoidance is not possible, devise a strategy ahead of time for dealing with these situations or people so that your anger will either be reduced or eliminated. Perhaps the most beneficial long-term result of analyzing your log is to learn *why* certain events, situations, issues, or people cause you to experience anger.

Don't Always Assume the Worst. We live in an imperfect world. People may say or do something that you find offensive without anticipating, realizing, or understanding that they hurt your feelings. Assume normalcy; rather than becoming angry at an ambiguous or inadvertent remark or act, assume that the offending party did not want to cause you distress, did not know you would become angry, and wants to get along with you.

Opening the Valve On the Pressure Cooker. There are various ways of releasing the anger that may build within you at the workplace. Physical activity—sports, exercise, or simply walking—is a healthy way to dispatch some of those angry beasts. For some, exertion is a way to release hostility.

Sports may also be a wonderful distraction. To the extent that most sports demand some degree of concentration, you cannot be thinking about your anger or its source while participating. People have reported to us that they often feel much less angry and uptight after playing tennis, handball, or golf.

Some people have had success in releasing their anger by writing a letter to the offending party explaining precisely what he or she does or has done that bothers them. If you choose to write a letter, indulge yourself; fantasize with glee over everything you would like to say and do to the individual. *Do not send the letter.* The simple act of expressing your anger on paper may dispel some of its force.

Use Your Support Network. Share your feelings of anger and its causes with a trusted colleague, spouse, or friend. Talk, scream, holler, cry. Having someone who will listen to your concerns and be sympathetic to your plight will help defuse some of your anger and hurt while also reminding you that there are people who care a great deal about your welfare. Such reminders should help you keep the issues causing your anger in perspective.

Protect and Expand Your Sources of Pleasure. Harry Levinson's book *Executive Stress* makes the excellent point that mentally healthy working people have many sources of pleasure in life.[6] Diversify, just like corporate America. Seek pleasure and a sense of efficacy outside the workplace in a variety of pursuits and activities that are interesting and enjoyable to you. Numerous sources of gratification should make your anger seem less encompassing

---

6. Harry Levinson, *Executive Stress* (New York: Mentor Books, New American Library, 1985).

and less threatening. The pleasure and self-esteem you derive from family, hobbies, service clubs, travel, and recreational activities can buffer or dilute the negative effects of anger, even keep it at bay.

Without this balance in your life, work assumes entirely too important a role. If your self-esteem, sense of identity, and pleasure are based solely on your work, any disruption there, no matter how minor, any setback, no matter how mild, any threat to your success, no matter how minuscule, has potentially devastating consequences.

The STLFT Process. STLFTs are, as we suggested in our chapter on boredom, phenomenal pleasure-givers and balance-keepers. Looking forward to a trip, delighting in the brochures, selecting a hotel, and deciding at which restaurants to gorge yourself can sometimes be more fun than the trip itself. These pleasant thoughts can remove the fangs from the sharp bite of anger. If you think you are going to have an anxiety- and anger-producing day, balance that foreboding with thoughts of fun-filled activities with friends: going to dinner, taking in a movie, or playing tennis. Instead of becoming a raging bull, shy mouse, omnivorous shark, or harboring a serpent in your bosom, let STLFTs help turn those beasts into pussy cats.

Give Me the Wisdom to Know the Difference. Some sources of your anger may be beyond your control—anger at rush-hour traffic, rejection by a client, cutbacks during a recession, a declining stock market. Try to accept the conditions that are inherent to your workplace and cannot be changed. If you are in sales, for instance, you must accept a degree of rejection: it goes with the territory. If you are a stockbroker, you must assume—and accept the fact—that some of your clients will occasionally criticize your judgment, even find a new broker. If you are an infallible stockpicker, your brain should be donated to science.

If you cannot accept the potential anger-producing elements that are inherent in your job, you should probably think about making a change. Some jobs may simply not be amenable to your personality and predilections.

Before taking the major step of changing jobs or professions, however, you may wish to discuss the entire matter with a counselor, psychologist, or psychiatrist. He or she may help you to understand better the relationship between your job and your anger, as well as help you to make a healthy new choice.

It is also possible that the ultimate source of the anger you experience at work lies in your personal life. We make a false division when we talk about workplace problems and personal problems; we are holistic organisms. Our working lives and our private lives are inextricably intertwined; what happens in one deeply affects the other. Again, a trained professional can help you understand if the anger you feel at work has its source in a wholly different place.

What to Do When Confronted by an Angry Employee

While many of our recommendations for exorcising anger are applicable for managers and bosses dealing with a disgruntled or angry employee, we wish to add several additional items:

Try to Anticipate and Detour any Potentially Angry Collision Before It Takes Place.   If you observe, for instance, that an employee seems disturbed at something that is occurring in your unit, if you hear someone grousing, or if you simply have a hunch that someone is smoldering inside, be proactive instead of reactive and ask to talk privately with the individual.

Once in your office, explain that you do not wish to pry, but that you have noticed that something seems awry and that, if at all possible, you would like to help. Addressing the source of the employee's anger may avert a belligerent confrontation.

Even if you cannot resolve the source of the problem or change the employee's mind, simply talking and listening about the situation, showing that you care, may be enough to assuage his or her ruffled feelings.

Resist the Urge to Respond to Anger With Anger.   Most often, anger only begets more anger. Your energy should be spent on listening, trying to identify the source of the anger, and finding a solution for the employee's problem.

Do Not Make a Knee-Jerk Reaction.   An employee's anger is not always without cause or basis. Assume that the individual would not be angry unless something important happened to him or her. Do not trivialize the issue. Listen to what the employee has to say, cut through the angry presentation, and determine the merits of the issue that he or she is raising. You may find that the core issue— the real reason why the individual is angry—goes far beyond the specific stimulus for the current outburst.

Evaluate the Issue Being Raised.   Is it a legitimate issue? Should I accede to the wishes of the disgruntled employee? If I do so, what effect will this have on the overall morale and productivity of the unit?

If you cannot grant the employee's wishes, explain your rationale so that your decision does not seem to be arbitrary.

Do Not Dread Such Encounters.   While dealing with an angry employee may not be quite as thrilling as winning the lottery, it need not be something that you dread. Look upon such confrontation as an opportunity to show your subordinates that you really care about their problems, that what they think and feel is of concern to you, and that their growth, development, and happiness at work are important to you.

Managers too, we hasten to add, have a right to feel anger. However, it must be expressed in an appropriate manner so that your future relationship with an employee will not be adversely affected. After you have expressed your feelings, put the issue behind you.

ANGER IS NOT A FOUR-LETTER WORD

Although the ice age of American management appears to be thawing, in the minds of many people work is invariably associated with cool and calm reason, detached and hard reality, and objective and scientific decision making. This kind of thinking, however, fails to acknowledge the emotional dimension of human nature. Anger is an emotion that virtually everyone experiences periodically; totally suppressing any expression of it in order to preserve the "professionalism" of the workplace does not seem like a healthy idea to us.

Some innovative firms have introduced employee assistance programs (EAPs) to help workers manage a host of problems ranging from drug abuse to anger. EAPs are designed to go one step beyond the traditional role played by employee relations divisions located within personnel departments. EAPs have trained counselors who help managers and employees, in complete confidence, to address the sources of and to find solutions for emotional, psychological, or family problems.

EAPs recognize that it is unrealistic to expect workers to leave all emotional, psychological, or personal problems in the parking lot when they arrive in the morning. These assistance programs are also good for business. As one human resources manager who works for a corporate EAP serving over 2,000 employees remarked: "EAPs have developed because of the recognition that feelings affect the ability of employees to perform their duties."

A work environment that sanctions the expression of negative feelings is consistent with workhealth. If negative emotions are precluded, positive emotions may be limited as well.

While we have dwelt in this chapter on anger as a negative emotion, we wish to suggest that it may also be a positive stimulus for all working people. Anger is capable of producing great energy, which in turn can be used to become more effective, productive, determined, and efficient. Bjorn Borg, five-time Wimbledon champion, is a case in point. Instead of reacting with pointless emotional outbursts, temper tantrums, and thrown racquets when a questionable call went against him, Borg transformed his anger into greater resolution and tenacity, heightened concentration and commitment, and, of course, better tennis.

Anger can provide energy and motivation for you to prove that someone has misjudged you, that you are capable of meeting the loftiest standards; it can provoke you to work harder to prove that you deserve a raise or promotion or bonus. Anger can stimulate you to remove impediments to your progress and give you the added strength needed to achieve what you know you are capable of achieving.

Anger can also be the start of a process of conflict resolution. It forces you to look at the sources, real or imagined, of your discontent and encourages you to address them.

Anger at times is a way of expressing righteous displeasure. It may provoke you to protect your values, assert your independence, and maintain your dignity and self-esteem.

Anger can be a catalyst for change, change within yourself or your environment. It can be a powerful signal that you should reappraise your understanding of yourself and your relationships with colleagues, as well as the suitability and appropriateness of your workplace surroundings and responsibilities. Anger may be the first warning that you and your job are not a good fit.

In an ideal world perhaps anger would not exist. People would immediately understand what was right and would do the right thing simply because it was right. We would never have to raise our voices, flex our muscles, take deep breaths, or lose our tempers.

All this is moot, of course, for we do not inhabit utopian digs. Since anger is a human emotion and since humans are fallible, it will be present anywhere there are people. There are no easy rules for determining when expressing anger is appropriate or even useful; each instance must be evaluated in its own terms. We have tried in this chapter to help you understand why anger occurs, how to confront, control, and express it, and how to make it work for you. Transforming our words into positive, resolute action is up to you.

Chapter Eight
"I Ain't Got Nobody"
Feeling Disconnected at Work

"Only connect . . ."

E. M. Forster, *Howards End*

O ne of the great joys of work has nothing to do with money, power, or prestige; it has to do with people. It is the pleasure derived from meeting people, building relationships, forming friendships, and experiencing companionship; it is the enjoyment and good feeling we get from working with others and sharing with them our thoughts and feelings, our hopes and fears.

For numerous people, however, the joys derived from socialization at work are minimal or nonexistent. Instead of interacting with others, these individuals remain isolated, alienated, and estranged. Instead of building relationships, they build walls that separate themselves from colleagues. Sometimes the isolation is unwittingly self-imposed; sometimes it is imposed upon them. In either case, the enormous personal and professional benefits obtained from connecting with others—the exhilaration of comradeship—is denied, and work becomes a sterile, lonely experience.

Consider the following composite scenarios and note if you recognize yourself or someone with whom you work.

Scenario 1.   Steve arrives at the planning committee meeting late. He has had two days that would make living on one of the inner circles of Dante's inferno look attractive: sick children, appointments, deadlines, project reports, and never-ending phone calls have made preparation for this meeting, once a priority, a wistful dream. The debate among his colleagues is intense—a healthy, heated, professional exchange. Having nothing to contribute and barely able to understand half of what is said, he feels alone and disconnected from the group, an outsider. Worse yet, immediately after the meeting his colleagues continue to ignore him as they do a postmortem on the session. He feels like the star of *The Invisible Man*.

Scenario 2.   Every time Joy tries to develop a relationship with people at work, they seem to react with coolness. She is rarely invited to join her colleagues for lunch; she knows some of them go for drinks after work, but somehow they forget to invite her. Conversations seem to conclude shortly after her contributions. She is convinced that if someone looked up *wallflower* in the dictionary, her picture would be there.

She decides to become proactive. She invites several colleagues to her place for a light dinner, but somehow they all have other commitments. She now decides to act more aggressively, but that only makes her feel uncomfortable. She just does not seem to fit in.

Scenario 3.   Mike desperately wants to be a part of the action at work, but he never seems to get assigned to important committees or asked at important moments for "your input," "your thoughts," or "your ideas." Mike feels passionately about his job and the mission of his company, but his colleagues fail to recognize his commitment. In fact, at his last performance review they said that he was not a team player, often disagreed with people, and never pitched in to help others. Despite Mike's hard work, his colleagues and boss seem to work around him, over him, by him, but never with him.

THE PROBLEM

Being Present but Disconnected

In the past, management-science theorists used the assembly-line worker as their model for isolation and insulation in the workplace; an individual who worked in proximity to others but was a single entity separate from everyone else.

Today that model has been expanded to include non–job-specific categories. The outsiders of the 1990s have set themselves apart largely because of personality characteristics, work attitudes and behaviors, and personal philosophies. They are, like the individuals in the scenarios above, shunned or ignored by colleagues and are rarely asked for their ideas, inputs, or opinions. Such people may work near others, but for all practical purposes they work alone, assembly-line workers recast.

The Costs of Being Disconnected

Disconnected people often do not enjoy work. They would like to have their social needs fulfilled by being part of a group, but their behaviors or attitudes often get in the way. Sometimes they are openly shunned and are simply never included in the social network. Sometimes they are excluded in a more covert and subtle fashion: people may pay lip service to what disconnected individuals have to say without giving their ideas serious attention.

When disconnected people try to become part of a group—which may entail swallowing their pride and making a significant effort to reach out to others—they often come away with frostbitten fingers. It is little wonder that they feel hurt, humiliated, rejected, and angry. Some may respond with hostility, which, of course, only serves to harden their colleagues' convictions. Others may respond by acting in a manner that is not natural to them; this also turns people off. Still others may respond by turning inward, increasing their isolation, and building higher and higher the walls of separation. Why continue to risk, they reason, the embarrassment and pain of rejection?

Ultimately, everyone loses. The disconnected employee loses because he or she remains frustrated and unhappy. The company loses because when an individual is alienated a valuable human resource is probably lost. Finally, coworkers and managers lose because a strained or awkward climate may emerge at work, making everyone feel uncomfortable.

WHY CONNECTIONS BREAK

There are numerous reasons why people find it difficult to form relationships at work or why those relationships are short-lived. We believe that the majority of these reasons are either *task-related*—based on the way an individual approaches his or her job—or *interpersonal*—based on the way an individual interacts with colleagues. However, it is difficult, perhaps even false, to try to separate an individual's attitude toward work from his or her attitude toward colleagues. The two—work and colleagues, tasks and the people who complete the tasks—are inextricably meshed.

Socrates said over 2,000 years ago that the basis of all knowledge is self-knowledge. Unfortunately, many individuals who have not been able to form relationships at work refuse to consider that they may be the cause of the problem. They refuse to look candidly at themselves, to examine the bases of their behaviors and attitudes, or to consider how they affect others. While inner reflection may shatter the illusions they have about themselves as being witty, sexy, or brilliant, it may also help them to understand why they are alone and isolated at work or why their relationships are short-lived.

As we have noted in our previous books, there are certain common task-related and interpersonal attitudes, behaviors, and philosophies that impede individuals from forming relationships at work. We hope that reviewing them with honesty and candor will both increase your self-awareness and suggest your possible complicity in the problem you may be having at work.

Bad Citizenship. Some people behave selfishly at work, indulging their every whim and desire without regard to others. Whether it is a trivial or a significant incident, their modus operandi is always the same: doing only what pleases themselves and ignoring the welfare or comfort of their colleagues. Among the more common practices of such individuals are the following:

• Refusing to do any task that is not expressly specified in their job descriptions.

• Refusing to help, pinch-hit, or pitch in when extra assistance is needed.

• Hoarding supplies that belong to an entire office or unit.

• Declining to volunteer for any task or assignment, even in an emergency.

• Failing to take messages for colleagues.

• Ignoring the dictates of common politeness; for example, taking all but the last centimeter of coffee to avoid making a fresh pot, setting the copy machine at 100 and failing to clear it for the next user, leaving a project or party immediately to avoid cleanup work.

Bad citizens are quickly spotted and assiduously avoided. They are not likely to be invited to serve on group projects or included in the social structure at work.

My World Only.   A successful and harmonious workplace is built on mutual understanding and assistance. Some people, however, see the significance of their jobs only and have little regard for the needs of others or even for the welfare of the firm. When colleagues ask them for advice, they give it as begrudgingly as Silas Marner would have given away one of his coins. When asked for help on work-related problems, their first inclination is to say, "I really don't know much about that." When coworkers share professional problems, they respond with one-upsmanship: "So your assignment is giving you a headache. My job is giving me a brain tumor." The concept of give-and-take or reciprocity is totally foreign to their thinking.

My Way Is Best.   There exists a particularly difficult type of individual in the workplace whose signature is, "If you can't do it my way, playing by my rules, then I refuse to work with you."

When people with this attitude suggest ideas that are rejected at meetings, they sulk, brood, and mumble words of discontent. They find it difficult, if not impossible, to refine, revise, tailor, alter, or adapt their original ideas based on the suggestions of others. They are islands unto themselves, refusing to compromise or strike a balance with the wishes of others. The bubonic plague would be a better partner on a group project.

The irony of the "My Way Is Best" people is that they fail to understand why they remain disconnected. They are convinced that they are trying their best, giving their all, and, perhaps most important, that they are right. Unfortunately, they are never witnesses to their own behavior; they see only the detrimental effect it has on their relationships with others.

Mother Stompers.   Another delightful type of workplace creature is the super-competitive fast tracker who would gladly step on his or her own mother to get ahead. These individuals will steal a colleague's ideas, usurp authority when they can, and poach on the successes of their coworkers. They often disregard the needs of their colleagues while fawning obsequiously to the people who possess the rewards they covet, their bosses. To their bosses, of course, they profess undying loyalty and total commitment; their coworkers, however, are inconsequential, mere bumps on their road to greatness. Mother Stompers are not difficult for colleagues or superiors to identify, for their very rapaciousness makes them obvious.

External Attributers.   "It's Not My Fault." These individuals, among the least tolerated in the workplace, refuse to take responsibility for their mistakes or failures. With a dexterity that would make Houdini envious, they will slip out of accountability and shamelessly shift responsibility for their misdeeds onto the shoulders of colleagues. Honesty, sincerity, dependability, and accountability have little place in their self-serving worlds.

Being Blind to Others.   Some individuals—too many, we fear—are grossly insensitive to the people around them. They use sexist language ("We have a great group of girls in the office"), tell off-color jokes, and think of colleagues in terms of racial, ethnic, or cultural stereotypes. They may not always realize the impact of their words and attitudes or intend to offend others, but ignorance is not a defense for their conduct.

Less obnoxious but still culpable are those individuals who are blind to the needs of their colleagues. There are times when a coworker needs a shoulder to cry on, a friend who will understand, a person who will sympathize, or someone who will simply give him or her a kind word. Some insensitive individuals, however, consider gentleness, tenderness, or kindness as a sign of weakness. They refuse to respond to the needs of others in a caring, humane fashion.

People who are insensitive or blind to the feelings and wishes of their colleagues fail to realize that showing kindness and consideration is a basic way to connect with others. "Thank you" builds bridges; "I'm sorry" makes one human. Offering a compliment or a helping hand, admitting a mistake, correcting a wrong, and rectifying an oversight are the blueprints for creating relationships at work.

While these are several of the major reasons for failing to connect with others at work, the first seven chapters of this book discuss problems that may also prevent you from forming relationships. For instance, failing to recognize the accomplishments of others, missing the opportunity to offer positive reinforcement and support, will not ingratiate an individual with his or her peers. Feeling bored drains one's energy and dulls one's senses so that it becomes difficult to reach out and respond with sensitivity to others. The individual who is preoccupied with attaining or managing success may be more likely to relegate the importance of friendship and kindness to a low place in his or her hierarchy of values. Feeling shy, intimidated, or vulnerable is also a major obstacle to forming relationships; unless one has the courage and confidence to reach out, connections become impossible. Inappropriately expressed anger, of course, erects an immediate barrier to colleagues; it estranges and alienates at the very time that an individual may be in great need of assistance and comfort. We hope that our attempts to help you manage those negative feelings and emotions will assist you in building relationships with colleagues.

Do You Possess the Skills to Connect?

Here is a brief quiz that assesses the extent to which you are likely to develop healthy, functional, and meaningful relationships at work. Although this quiz has not been psychometrically validated, we believe that it should give you some preliminary insight into your likelihood of connecting with others at work.

	Strongly Disagree	Disagree	Neither Agree nor Disagree	Agree	Strongly Agree
1. I find it easy to make friends at work.	1	2	3	4	5
2. Others ask for my ideas and input.	1	2	3	4	5
3. When I speak at meetings, people seem to listen closely.	1	2	3	4	5
4. I tend to do other people favors at work.	1	2	3	4	5
5. People confide in me.	1	2	3	4	5
6. I tend to confide in others, though with care.	1	2	3	4	5
7. I am very sensitive to the needs of people with whom I work.	1	2	3	4	5
8. People tell me that I am an understanding person.	1	2	3	4	5
9. I have little difficulty giving colleagues compliments they deserve.	1	2	3	4	5

	Strongly Disagree	Disagree	Neither Agree nor Disagree	Agree	Strongly Agree
10. I have no problem telling others they have not done a good job.	1	2	3	4	5
11. When I give negative feedback, colleagues seem to take it well.	1	2	3	4	5
12. I care about the people with whom I work.	1	2	3	4	5
13. I try to share resources with others at work.	1	2	3	4	5
14. I work hard to develop trusting relationships at work.	1	2	3	4	5
15. People at work seem to enjoy my company.	1	2	3	4	5
16. I laugh a lot with colleagues at work.	1	2	3	4	5
17. People respect me for the job I do.	1	2	3	4	5
18. I find it easy to identify with the workplace problems of others.	1	2	3	4	5
19. I find it easy to empathize with the personal problems of colleagues.	1	2	3	4	5
20. I am genuinely interested in the work of others.	1	2	3	4	5
21. I am genuinely interested in the nonworkplace issues discussed by my colleagues.	1	2	3	4	5

	Strongly Disagree	Disagree	Neither Agree nor Disagree	Agree	Strongly Agree
22. I find it easy to ask others if they need help or assistance.	1	2	3	4	5
23. I enjoy offering my help and assistance to others at work.	1	2	3	4	5
24. I find it easy to ask for help at work when I am facing a problem.	1	2	3	4	5
25. I try to avoid making judgments about others until I have enough information.	1	2	3	4	5
26. I work hard at trying to determine how colleagues perceive me.	1	2	3	4	5
27. I ask colleagues how they perceive me.	1	2	3	4	5
28. I try to be fair in my dealings with others at work.	1	2	3	4	5
29. If there is a party at work, I will stay until the end to help clean up the mess.	1	2	3	4	5
30. I tend to use different interpersonal styles for different situations I face at work.	1	2	3	4	5

Add up the numbers you have circled. Scores can range from a low of 30 points to a high of 150 points. The higher your score, the more likely it is that you are currently successfully connecting with others at work or that you have the potential for building sound relationships.

If your score was not as high as you had wished, or if you have a high overall score but were low on one or several questions, you may find the recommendations in this chapter useful. If you are satisfied with your score, perhaps we can suggest several ways to help others who are struggling to create relationships at work.

BECOMING CONNECTED AT WORK

Eleven Ways to Build Relationships

Creating supportive and fulfilling relationships at work generally does not demand draconian measures or Herculean efforts. The basic methods that may be employed for connecting with colleagues are, we believe, direct, relatively uncomplicated, and thoroughly doable.

1. What Can I Do to Help? In one company we observed, the CEO created an organizational mode of conduct built around the question, "What can I do to help?" The expectation was that each person in the company would take the time and initiative to ask his or her colleagues this question. When employees finished a job early and had some time to spare, it was assumed that they would ask coworkers or managers if they needed any assistance. This simple question, asked in a sincere manner, became an incredibly successful method for building sound and productive relationships in the firm.

We recommend asking this question when appropriate, for the offer of assistance creates a structure around which relationships can emerge and be maintained. If a person responds, "I need help getting this presentation together," then the two of you have informally created a work group, a structural entity with which you are now affiliated. Such structures often lead to increased caring, listening, empathy, and, finally, relationships.

2. Connect with Favors. Doing favors for colleagues is part of the give-and-take of the workplace. Doctors frequently cover one another's patients, employees pinch-hit on projects when a colleague is ill or on vacation, CEOs take phone messages when a secretary is momentarily absent. These citizenship behaviors are at the heart of building and maintaining social and professional relationships on the job.

Look around your workplace and identify a person who, regardless of official rank, fills in for a sick coworker, cleans the mess after an office party, offers to make the coffee, takes phone messages for colleagues, or volunteers to get someone more copy paper so that he or she can continue working to meet a deadline. We suspect that this individual relates well to others, is a part of the social network in the office, is often asked for his or her opinion on an issue, has numerous friends, and is cherished by his or her coworkers and superiors.

Furthermore, good citizens do not do favors on a quid pro quo basis. They do not keep detailed records of debits and credits, hold a good deed over someone's head for a future favor, or manipulate through favors. Rather they offer assistance out of a genuine conviction that this is the way that people can best serve and relate to one another, and that kindness and altruism have their own rewards.

3. Connect by Showing Interest.   Asking colleagues about their assignments, listening to their remarks about issues they are facing, and offering advice when asked—in essence, showing an interest in the work of colleagues—is an excellent way to build relationships.

The importance of understanding one another's work prompted one senior manager to have his staff make short presentations on upcoming and continuing projects during monthly staff meetings. Upon hearing a colleague's remarks, it was not uncommon for someone to say, "I'm interested in that issue as well. Why don't we get together?" The result was a cross-pollination that led to greater productivity; connections were formed and bridges were built.

4. Be Honest.   One of the best ways to establish a relationship is to be honest in your evaluation of a colleague. When a coworker asks for your opinion, assume that he or she is not trolling for a compliment but is genuinely seeking a candid answer. Although we believe that relationships that are not based on honesty are probably not worth having, we hasten to add that candor and tact are not mutually exclusive. We suggest the following guidelines for combining the two:

a. While organizational theory tells us to give feedback, good or bad, soon after an event or behavior, diplomacy and common sense suggest that at times it may be best to wait for the right circumstances. If a colleague is obviously crestfallen over losing an account and asks for your opinion on precisely how he or she erred, you may wish to wait a day or two before giving your full response. An immediate "I'm sorry" may be a more effective antidote than a full explanation of how matters could have been handled differently.

b. Separate the person from the issue if the feedback is negative. In giving your opinion of a mishandled project or assignment, be sure to let your colleague understand that criticism of his or her work is not personal criticism. While our work may be vitally important, it is what we do, not what or who we are. Make it clear that you are evaluating one specific instance of a colleague's work and not the talent, commitment, or character of the individual.

c. If the feedback is negative, don't dwell exclusively on the negative. Under most circumstances, the privilege of criticizing comes with the responsibility to offer positive advice for rectifying a problem. If you wish to be a valued colleague, become part of the solution. You may also give balance to your criticism by reminding your colleague of all the sound and effective work that he or she has done.

Honesty should extend to all your interactions with colleagues. Consider our earlier example about lunch. How often, for instance, have coworkers said, "Let's have lunch" or "I'll stop by soon," without following through on their promises? How often have colleagues asked "How are you doing?" when you knew full well that they had virtually no concern over the state of your physical or emotional health? Insincere prattle, false declarations, and phony questions do little to establish meaningful relationships at work; in fact, they are often smoke screens behind which people hide.

If you wish to have lunch with someone, give a specific time and place when you offer the invitation. If you declare that you will visit someone's office, be sure to do so. When you ask a colleague "How are you?" let him or her know that you are not simply asking a perfunctory question. Look the person in the eye when you make the inquiry, stop what you are doing, and wait for a response.

5. Connect by Sharing Resources. One way to help a colleague solve a problem is to share information and resources with him or her. If you read an article that you think might be of value to a coworker, send it to him or her. If you have an idea that might be helpful or hear something that might be relevant to a colleague's work, share the idea or the information. If another department is short staffed or in need of extra equipment and you are in a position to help, offer assistance. You will create grateful friends while improving the overall performance of your company.

6. Connect with Excellent Job Performance. In this chapter, we have already discussed the detrimental effects of certain workplace attitudes, behaviors, and philosophies on one's ability to form relationships (see "Why Connections Break"). While inherently damaging, those attitudes, behaviors, and philosophies are often closely related to poor job performance, which may also alienate colleagues. There are numerous poses, postures, and practices—in addition to those we have already suggested—that may have become so much a part of an individual's workplace repertoire that he or she no longer realizes their negative impact:

- Blaming others for your mistakes.
- Consistently being late for meetings.
- Keeping colleagues waiting over 10 minutes for appointments. The tacit message is, "It's all right for you to wait because my time is more important than your time."
- Delegating work that should be done by you.

- Consistently canceling appointments and meetings at the last minute.
- Attending meetings without doing your homework.
- Waiting until the last minute to complete an important assignment or to prepare for a major event. This often creates anxiety in colleagues who depend on your work.
- Consistently failing to pull your weight on group projects or in the office.
- Allowing assignments to fall through the proverbial cracks.
- Being a rerouter. We know of one manager who used to defer all requests made of him to other managers in the organization. He was in sales, and when a sales complaint came to him, he would say, "Go to production with that; it is really their problem." When a client called because an order was shipped late, he would have the client call shipping to find out what happened. When someone requested sales figures, he would refer them to billing. Although this particular individual could not be fired for political reasons, he quickly became the most isolated person in the organization.

While any one or combination of these behaviors could very easily result in the loss of one's job, many individuals are skillful enough to know precisely how much they can do with impunity. While their brinkmanship may preserve their jobs, their conduct alienates their colleagues. If you are perceived as dilatory, a slacker, slipshod in your methods, unprofessional, a nonperformer, or a rerouter, you will quickly become persona non grata. Few people want to associate with such an individual; they do not think well of a coworker who does not take his or her job seriously and who does not consistently try to do quality work. Doing your job well and participating actively and responsibly in the life of your office and organization are among the most effective ways to connect with colleagues.

7. Be Sensitive to Your Colleagues. People with excellent interpersonal skills are sensitive to the preferences and aversions, the predilections and bêtes noires of their colleagues. Individuals who are able to form friendships at work are generally tuned in to the needs, moods, feelings, and values of coworkers.

You develop this sensitivity by listening and observing carefully. Learn how to "read" your colleagues; try to determine, for instance, when an individual needs someone to talk to and when a colleague should be left alone; when to make a joke and when to commiserate; when to take charge and when to back off. If a coworker or boss expresses either verbally or through body language that he or she is overworked, overextended, or experiencing stress, you may wish to ask, "What can I do to help?" If you observe that a colleague likes to work alone, respect those wishes; if you hear that a colleague would like to share an assignment, try to be accommodating.

Since our professional lives and our personal lives are closely related, it should not be surprising that colleagues will at times wish to talk about their families. Allow them to do this; in fact, you may wish to participate actively by asking them questions about their families. If the questions are broad, your colleagues will be able to set the level of detail and intimacy with which they feel comfortable. Asking about their families will send the message that you care about them as individuals and not simply as people with a workplace function.

There are no secret formulas to follow or magical potions to imbibe in order to increase your sensitivity; what is required is the willingness to look beyond yourself and the desire to relate to and assist others.

8. Trust Your Colleagues.   We realize that there are many battle-scarred veterans in the work force who have trusted others only to find that their confidence had been misplaced. Mistrust, however, and the cynicism that often follows in its wake, will result in a self-imposed alienation. If you wish to form relationships, it is necessary to trust and to believe in people. We have several caveats and suggestions for establishing trusting relationships:

• Trust must be mutual for a sound relationship to exist. Mutual trust, however, does not generally develop quickly. Be cautious and deliberate determining in whom you can confide, especially when you are new on a job or in a new situation. Allow the actions of colleagues to dictate whether they are reliable and dependable.

• Look for patterns of conduct in your colleagues. If a coworker reveals a piece of confidential information about another colleague to you, it is reasonable to assume that he or she will also reveal private information about you to other colleagues. If a coworker breaks promises or commitments to others, do not expect to be spared yourself.

• Recognize that trust and risk go hand in hand. Believing in another person, revealing your private thoughts and feelings, and depending on someone else place you in a vulnerable position. We believe, however, that trusting others is a risk well worth taking, for playing it safe or trusting only yourself will generally prevent you from building relationships. And if you are betrayed, we hope that you will not adopt an isolationist posture. Diagnose where you misread the person or situation and try not to make the same mistake again.

9. Connect with Humor. Humor is a valuable method for starting a relationship or for becoming part of a group. People enjoy laughing and, we believe, desire the company of an upbeat individual who brings a smile to their lips. Humor is a wonderful icebreaker; it is an effective means for starting a conversation or for overcoming awkward situations. It is also a useful coping tool; being able to laugh at your own foibles and faux pas, being able to stand apart from yourself and see humor in embarrassing and disconcerting events, will help you to manage frustration, maintain an emotional equilibrium, and keep stress at arm's length. In short, humor will make you a more attractive person while helping you overcome some of the personal obstacles to establishing relationships.

If you do not feel comfortable telling jokes or making quips, let others do it for you. Cut out a humorous cartoon or an unusual news article, for instance, and share it at work. One caveat: Jokes at the expense of another—sexist, ethnic, religious, or racial jokes—are not humorous; they are offensive and demeaning and should always be avoided.

10. Be Fair. It may seem axiomatic, but people who are seen by their colleagues as fair and just are usually well liked and respected.

We wish to suggest several common ways to increase your fair-mindedness:

• Look at issues from multiple perspectives. Rarely are issues black and white; before making a judgment, listen and consider all sides and all aspects.

• Avoid premature value judgments. Do not make quick, knee-jerk reactions; instead, wait until all the facts are in, all the data have been collected, and all the evidence has been gathered and evaluated. Base your decisions on facts and evidence, not on someone's impressions. If you should change your mind about an issue, freely express your new opinion without embarrassment or reluctance; "a foolish consistency," as Ralph Waldo Emerson once said, "is the hobgoblin of little minds."

• Tell the truth. Few characteristics will make someone persona non grata more quickly than dishonesty. Honesty demands that your version of the truth remain the same for all colleagues and that you wear one face at work. Honesty sometimes demands that you give negative feedback to a colleague or become the bearer of bad news. Honesty may also demand admitting that you were wrong, made a mistake, or erred in judgment. Infallibility may be impossible, but honesty is not.

• Evaluate content first, content second, content third. Judgments should be based on the merits of a project, plan, projection, or idea and not on the personality of its author. If the most obnoxious person in the organization has a great idea, be the first to acknowledge his or her achievement.

• Let colleagues know what you are thinking. Allow your co-workers to see the bases of your judgments; tell them why you think or act in a particular fashion. This is especially important for managers. Explaining your rationale will help to avoid misunderstandings and possible resentment. Even if subordinates do not agree with your decision, their anger or opposition may be defused if they understand the bases for your actions.

11. Connect by Being You.   You are the most important person with whom to be honest. We have observed scores of people in the workplace who try to relate to colleagues by feigning interests, opinions, and life-styles that are not their own. We have seen conservative women try to relate to men by wearing provocative clothing, and men try to change their images by pouring on cologne that arrives five minutes before they do. The results have ranged from embarrassment to disaster.

If you prefer rock to classical music, or reading a book to smacking a tennis ball, accept that fact. If you believe the majority opinion or prevailing attitude in your office is wrong, say so albeit with diplomacy. In most instances, fakery, insincerity, and duplicity are easily sensed by others. What's more important, they will make you feel like a fraud. Let people accept you, warts and all.

Too Much of a Good Thing: When Connections Get Too Close

Although Mae West once observed, "Too much of a good thing is splendid," close relationships at work can elicit feelings as negative and problems as vexing as those accompanying the failure to form relationships. Some individuals, for instance, work so hard at forming and maintaining relationships and contacts that they ignore their job responsibilities. There are several easily identified species:

• *Homo Chatterus.* Some people spend most of their day chatting about anything and everything—the weather, children, politics, sun spots, Halley's comet, the price of bananas, depletion of the ozone layer, medieval conceptions of space and time, the color of a yak's milk (which is pink, by the way)—to anyone with a pair of ears. Indeed, their self-proclaimed expertise would humble Leonardo da Vinci and Einstein combined. Although they may initially form many associations, chatterers often do not wear well. Colleagues will frequently go out of their way to avoid their time-consuming prattle.

• *Networker Apiarius* ("Maintainer of the Beehive"). Some individuals spend the majority of each day building and rebuilding networks. They never miss a party, conference, meeting, or telephone call from someone they can add to the hive. They justify giving short shrift to their other tasks by claiming that they are "developing important relationships." Unfortunately, they see networking as an end in itself rather than a means to an end.

Like the *Homo Chatterus*, these modern-day Typhoid Marys are assiduously avoided by any colleague who is interested in substance rather than style, achievement rather than posing.

• *Ad Ultimum Bucca.* Some individuals insist on unburdening themselves to colleagues, revealing their most intimate secrets and desires; hence, their Latin name, "the Ultimate Mouthful." The desire to share everything and anything eventually leads to isolation; colleagues often feel uncomfortable hearing about the personal matters of these individuals, while the Ultimate Mouthfuls are, in turn, embarrassed at seeing colleagues who know so much about them.

If in a weak moment you are tempted to reveal a truly personal matter to a colleague, reflect on how you will feel about that colleague knowing this information a day from now, a week from now, or a year from now. While it is difficult to establish a rule of thumb for revealing personal thoughts and feelings, we believe in erring on the side of discretion.

Love Among the Filing Cabinets

Romantic involvement at work is a prime instance of the potentially negative fallout from relationships that are too close.[1] The workplace is a fertile environment for romance. Work takes bright, energetic people with similar interests and puts them in close proximity for half their waking hours. The pressure-cooker atmosphere of work, coping with unforeseen problems, the joy of victory, the agony of defeat—these all create close and intense bonds among people in short periods of time.

While we are realistic enough to know that romantic attachments between employees do occur, and while we know of couples working in the same office who have successfully combined a working

---

1. A brief portion of our discussion of romance at work also appears in *Transitions: Successful Strategies from Mid-Career to Retirement* (*"Surviving Your Employees' Divorce"*).

and a romantic relationship, we believe that combining romance and work is generally a bad idea—a very bad idea.

There is perhaps no feeling more fulfilling and wonderful than romance. We hasten to add, however, that there is perhaps no feeling more distracting than romance. This generally does not create a problem when you are able to divide your day between your romantic life and your work life. With an office romance, however, the two become intermingled and intertwined. When the source of your passion is physically nearby, directing your energy, attention, and concentration on assigned tasks becomes problematical. It can be difficult enough to put your love life on hold for eight hours a day. With an office romance, it becomes almost impossible.

While distraction at work is a problem, there is an even greater potential danger. Most romances, despite our initial illusions and the plots of Harlequin novels, eventually end, often with less than cordial feelings on the part of one or both parties. When the romance has taken place outside the workplace, it is generally not difficult to avoid seeing or talking to each other. When the liaison is with a colleague, however, it is virtually impossible to avoid encounters or interactions. While this may result in mutual embarrassment or an awkward atmosphere, the difficulty is compounded when jobs demand cooperation and collaboration between both parties. A romance turned sour can quickly become a productivity problem and an office morale disaster.

While romantic involvement between peers is tricky business, it is even more dangerous when a supervisor and his or her subordinate have a liaison. A supervisor, for example, may be perceived as showing favoritism to the subordinate with whom he or she is involved. Whether favoritism or preferential treatment has, in fact, taken place is a moot point—the perception that it has occurred is enough to create a morale problem among other employees in the unit. A morale problem, in turn, may quickly become a productivity problem that will attract the unwanted attention of superiors.

Furthermore, coworkers will often avoid a colleague who is having a romantic relationship with a supervisor, fearing that anything they say will be quickly transmitted to their boss. Ironically, a relationship that is too close may cause the isolation of an individual from his or her colleagues.

Humans, of course, are not automatons; it is much easier to state that romance at work should be avoided than it is to follow that advice. Short of recommending a cold shower, we have several suggestions for quenching the romantic fires before they are ignited:

Do Not Play Sexual Games. Some individuals unfortunately assume that working with members of the opposite gender automatically requires them to play various types of flirtatious and sexual games. We know of one male manager, for instance, who would ask his secretary or female managers to visit him in his office after working hours. When they asked, "What work will we be doing?" he would reply, "Oh, we'll think of something." We also know of a woman manager who closed her office door after a male colleague entered, stood in front of him, gently cuffed her hands over his shoulders, and said, "You have a great body. You don't need shoulder pads in your suits."

Sexual innuendoes, double entendres, implied assignations, verbal intimacy, bawdy remarks, and sexually aggressive behavior are always out of place. It is naive to think that you can play these games just for the fun of it; they send the very definite message that you are ready for a more intimate relationship. Furthermore, such remarks and behaviors are unprofessional and offensive.

Discourage Romantic or Sexual Advances. If you think that someone is "coming on" to you, let him or her know immediately that you are not interested. One polite and effective way of doing this is to let the individual know that you are happily married or that you are involved with a significant other. A picture of your loved one displayed on your desk may silently make a similar statement.

Avoid Discussing Sexual Matters. These could include romantic office gossip, what really happens when you call a 1–900 number, or intimate relationships you or others have had. If the conversation should turn in any of these directions, reroute or terminate it. If the person with whom you are speaking has any sensitivity, he or she will understand that you do not wish to discuss such matters.

Keep Your Hands to Yourself. Numerous offices have "touchy-feely" atmospheres in which people casually put an arm around a colleague's shoulder or give a hug and kiss to someone who lands a major account. If you know your audience and you are *certain* that your gestures will be interpreted as nothing more than friendly support, you are probably on safe ground making such physical connections. If, however, you do not know the individual well, if you are not sure how he or she will react, or if you are not certain how your gestures will be interpreted, discretion is advisable.

Keep Your Eyes on Business. Staring or ogling at an attractive coworker or at a part of his or her anatomy is a demeaning and dehumanizing gesture. People generally stare at things: when you stare at or ogle a person, it tends to reduce that individual to a sexual object. While this is offensive to the person who is being stared at, it also sends the signal to others that you may be looking for a sexual or romantic liaison.

Keep Your Mouth on Business. Lewd jokes (which are almost always at the expense of women), speculation on someone's sexual prowess, or attempts at sexual wit ("If I told you that you had a beautiful body, would you hold it against me?"), while inherently unprofessional, often have the same effect as staring at or drooling over a colleague's appearance; they give the impression that you may be receptive to establishing a sexual or romantic relationship.

Carefully Regulate Any Drinking with Colleagues. We realize that coworkers will sometimes have a drink together after working hours, during lunch, or at an office party. Unfortunately, as drinking increases, self-management weakens. The frequent result is inappropriate or embarrassing words and gestures that may be hard to live down. In the contemporary workplace, you will be judged on your words and behaviors and not on the innocence of your intentions.

I'VE TRIED BUT I STILL CANNOT
FORM RELATIONSHIPS

We have recommended throughout this chapter the importance of taking resolute action on your own behalf to forge relationships at work. If you have tried various solutions to the problem over a reasonable period of time and none has worked, then perhaps the fit between you and your coworkers, you and your boss, or you and your job is improper. It is possible that you are working with and for people whose view of the world is so radically differently from your own—different values, different goals, different philosophies—that trying to establish relationships is quixotic. It is also possible that your job is so unsuitable for you that you are not succeeding at it, which, as we noted earlier, may make it difficult to form relationships. If these conditions exist, it is probably advisable to transfer to a different office or to find another job. This, of course, should only be done after trying the various suggestions we have made for connecting and after carefully analyzing your personal situation.

You may want to solicit the guidance of others to help you analyze your relationships or lack thereof. You may wish, for instance, to have a confidential discussion with your boss or a trusted colleague. You may want to visit someone in human resources management, such as an employee-relations counselor, to discuss your inability to form relationships with coworkers. A mentor in or out of your firm may also offer valuable guidance. If you feel uncomfortable asking colleagues or friends for this type of advice, consider seeking professional counseling. In any event, *you* hold the key to the solution. Nothing will change unless *you* make it change.

If you are working exclusively or even largely for a paycheck, we think that you are selling yourself short. Besides being a source of income, work should be personally enjoyable, fulfilling, and enriching. One of the greatest sources for these qualities rests in our relationships with our colleagues. Colleagues can be a strong source of professional support, supplying guidance and assistance; they can function as a buffer against an angry boss, a disgruntled client, or simply a bad day; they can provide stability against the vicissitudes of the workplace; they can add laughter, cheerfulness, and good humor to our lives; they can help us rise to the full level of our talents; they can supply the emotional and personal support that may be missing in other parts of our lives. Strong, honest, and caring relationships at work are as important as any aspect of our professional lives.

Chapter Nine
Workhealth and Workplay

W *ork Is Not A Four-Letter Word* is about managing negative emotions and feelings at work. A book, however, can only analyze, inform, advise, and encourage. It cannot act; only you can do that. The good news is that there is no one more interested in your welfare than you; the bad news, if you can call it that, is that all the responsibility is yours.

THE IMPORTANCE OF WORK

Work is a meaningful part of our lives. It provides us with the pleasure and excitement that comes from meeting challenges: being confronted with a difficult assignment or problem, devising an approach for attacking or solving it, and completing the task successfully. Work helps us to become more interesting and engaging people; it encourages us to look beyond and out of ourselves and to learn from the richness of our environment. Work gives us the opportunity to have pride in ourselves and what we do; it provides us with a source for self-esteem and a sense of fulfillment. It allows us to feel productive and efficacious, to feel like a valued member of society. Work also helps us to satisfy our social needs; humans are gregarious creatures who need the friendships and interactions that work provides. So valuable an experience is work that we suspect that most people would continue with their jobs even if they won the lottery and did not have to work for financial reasons.

Finally, and perhaps most importantly, work is a wonderful way to learn about ourselves—to determine our strengths and weaknesses, our predilections and prejudices; to find out what satisfies us and what leaves us with a feeling that there must be more; to learn what turns us on, turns us off, or turns us inside out. Joseph Conrad, the early twentieth-century author of *Lord Jim* and *Heart of Darkness*, once remarked that he did not like work. What he liked, he continued, was what was *in* the work: the opportunity it gave him to find himself. We believe his observation is no less true today.

Workhealth and Laughter

Although the importance of work makes it serious business—perhaps *because* work is so important and serious—it is vital to be able to laugh at ourselves, our follies, foibles, and mistakes. Humans, according to Mark Twain, are the only creatures in the animal kingdom who laugh or who have need to laugh.

We know of one college history professor who begins every class with a pun, comic impersonation of a historical figure, or quick joke. Although the students react to such antics with groans, this practice, he believes, helps to create a relaxed and positive environment for learning. By removing some of the tension, self-consciousness, and uptightness often present in a classroom, he has established an atmosphere in which students do not find it difficult to respond to questions or to each other's remarks. "Sticking your neck out" is less of an issue since the instructor has already stuck his neck out. We also believe that the self-irony involved in such activities, the sense of not taking oneself so deadly seriously, is an important response to the seriousness of the workplace.

We have also been told about an incident that occurred at a large meeting of corporate middle managers with their CEO. While the CEO was talking about fairly heady stuff, an individual near him in the front row let out the mother of all sneezes: "Ahhhhhhhh-choooooooooooooo!" The CEO instantly stumbled backwards as if hit by a gale-force wind, while his facial expression was that of a man who had just lived through Hurricane Hugo. The audience and the sneezer burst out into peals of laughter and clapped their approval.

The CEO's sense of humor immediately won the favor of his audience; they now saw him not as an embodiment of a profit-and-loss statement but as a "real" person, one who did not take himself so seriously that he could not laugh at the incongruity of a situation. His impromptu comedy succeeded in removing the barrier between himself and his employees more effectively than anything we could invent.

You Can Have Your Cake

We have discussed throughout *Work Is Not a Four-Letter Word* the importance of your personal support group in helping you to control and resolve the negative feelings or emotions experienced at work. Your family, spouse, and friends are almost as vital to your success as the personal characteristics that you bring to the workplace.

We do not believe that an insuperable gulf, tension, or antagonism should exist between your personal life and your professional life or among the various roles you fulfill—employee, parent, spouse, friend. In fact, we think that the quality of our lives and our degree of workhealth increases when we are satisfying numerous roles and avoiding pigeonholing ourselves into playing one part exclusively or largely. We do not see why you cannot have your cake, eat it, and even stay slim; why you cannot achieve success in all your roles, at the workplace and at home, in your professional life and your personal life.

We think that the findings of a recent psychological study of women funded by the National Science Foundation is relevant to our discussion. Doctors Grace Baruch, Rosalind Barnett, and Caryl Rivers attempted in their research to answer the central question

"What contributes to a woman's sense of well-being?" They concluded that a woman's well-being is based on a feeling of "mastery," which consists largely of achievement at work, and "pleasure," which is associated with home and personal life. Their
findings challenge the time-worn but time-honored view that pleasure or the "feeling side of life" is the sole source of a woman's
well-being, as well as the either-or view of pitting home life against
work life that has been traditionally imposed on women: "A woman's well-being is enhanced when she takes on multiple roles. At
least by middle adulthood, the women who were involved in a
combination of roles—marriage, motherhood, and employment—
were the highest in well-being. . . . Clearly, work has a profound
effect on a woman's sense of self-worth, her feelings of being in
charge of her life, and her chances of avoiding depression and
anxiety."[1]

While this superb study focused on the well-being of women,
its conclusions seem to us to be relevant for men as well. In fact,
it is probably easier for men to assume multiple roles and to balance
their professional and personal lives, since society has traditionally
allowed men greater freedom than women in defining their roles
and interests and in avoiding the stultifying effects of rigid
classification.

Creativity and Workplay: Another Tool to Resolve
the Past and Manage the Future

We hope that when you are no longer plagued with negative feelings and emotions, you will be able to turn your attention to meeting the increasingly complex demands and challenges that virtually
all workers will face in the next decade. We believe that these new
demands and challenges will necessitate a greater amount of creativity than has been required at any time in our recent past.

Creativity is also one of the most effective antidotes for the negative feelings and emotions that we have discussed throughout

---

1. "Happiness Is a Good Job," *Working Woman* 8 (February 1983), pp. 75–78; this article
is adapted from *Lifeprints: New Patterns of Love and Work for Today's Women* by the same
authors.

Work Is Not a Four-Letter Word. These feelings and emotions, like old thought patterns, often become habitual. Creativity can empower you to break free of the old and take on the new; knowing that you can think more creatively, imaginatively, and expansively will impart both the confidence that you can resolve workplace problems and the methods for doing so.

Unfortunately, creativity in the workplace seems to be in short supply. Most workers, we are convinced, go about fulfilling their daily assignments and responsibilities in a routine, time-worn, and predictable fashion. Instead of looking at their work with fresh eyes, they are content to follow the procedures, methods, and practices of the past. Perhaps the following exercise will suggest the problem. Your task is to connect all nine dots below using only four straight lines, while not allowing your pen or pencil to leave the page.

```
•   •   •

•   •   •

•   •   •
```

Give up? The solution to the problem is to go *outside* of the physical boundaries established by the dots.

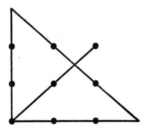

While this exercise obviously does not constitute a formal evaluation of one's imaginative powers, it does suggest our propensity for imposing limitations on ourselves. In fact, we think that most limitations are self-imposed. We are so accustomed to following the rules that we make up rules when none are given. We have been told so often to color inside the lines that we now do so by habit. Perhaps we may become so accustomed to experiencing negative feelings and emotions at work that we have given up trying to manage them.

As children we were much more creative and imaginative than we are as adults. Routine, habituation, the pressure to conform, and the rigidity of our educational system, unfortunately, have worked to wrench out of us the creativity that we once had.

One of the activities we engaged in as children that helped us to develop our creativity was play. When we played "make believe" and fantasy games—transforming objects such as sticks into rocket ships and space aliens, taking empty boxes and filling them with the stuff of our imaginations—we were developing our creative and imaginative powers.

Unfortunately, play—daydreaming, fantasizing, allowing our imaginations to wander without direction—seems to have little place in the workplace or in achieving workhealth. In a nation whose work habits are founded on the Protestant ethic, play seems like a silly and costly waste of time. Yet it is, we believe, a valuable method for regaining some of our lost creativity and dealing with current problems and future challenges. When we asked numerous creative people how, when, and where they get their imaginative ideas, most responded with phrases such as, "When I'm not concentrating on anything in particular," "When I let myself daydream," "When I let my mind roam," "When I'm listening to music or taking a walk." During such times, when we temporarily suspend our powers of reason and logic, our minds are allowed to break down the rigid categories we impose on reality and to make connections among disparate and widely divergent ideas.

Bruno Bettelheim, perhaps the foremost authority on the role of play in human development, describes our need for what he calls *Spielraum*, a German word that Bettelheim defines as "free scope, 'plenty of room'—to move not only one's elbows but also one's mind, to experiment with things and ideas at one's leisure, or, to put it colloquially, to toy with ideas."[2] It is during periods of *Spielraum*, when we take respite from our daily anxieties and tensions,

---

2. "The Importance of Play," *The Atlantic Monthly* 259 (March 1987), pp. 35-43.

our routines and regimentations, that the creativity we had as children is allowed to take center stage. It is when we give ourselves room—cut ourselves some slack—that the richness of our imagination is allowed to express itself.

In what may seem like an irony, it is the increasing demands of the workplace to find new solutions to problems and to achieve greater productivity that makes taking time for play so vitally important. Make mental R & R, daydreaming, fantasizing, woolgathering a part of your work agenda. Schedule into your day some time for walking, strolling, jogging, sitting on a park bench, driving in the country, listening to music, and watching children play.

One of the key elements in becoming more creative and imaginative is to resist the urge to use approaches, methods, and patterns of thinking that you have employed in the past. Instead, when confronted with a new task or old problem, let your mind roam freely so that you will be able to see new relationships, new connections, and new analogies between the requirements of the task or problem at hand and all that you have observed, all that you have read, and all that you have experienced. Creativity demands that you think in associative terms, that you find correlations, similarities, and kinships among even seemingly disparate ideas and approaches.

Any type of mental exercise that forces you to think expansively, that makes you look at reality in a new way, or that requires you to see connections among different experiences or ideas will help you develop your creative powers. You can find such exercises in a game book, or you can create them yourself.[3] You may wish, for instance, to look at a picture or a doodle and to give as many interpretations of what you see as you can. Rebuses or various word games will also stimulate you to see concepts, letters, numbers, and words in new and different ways. Creating your own metaphors or similes is another excellent method for developing

---

3. Three books that we have found especially useful in developing creativity are Eugene Raudsepp, *More Creative Growth Games* (New York: G.P. Putnam, 1980), Roger van Oech, *A Whack on the Side of the Head* (New York: Warner Books, 1983), and *A Kick in the Seat of the Pants* (New York: Harper & Row, 1986).

the ability to form links or associations among divergent items. For example, see how many comparisons you can make for each of the following:

- Working at my firm is like shopping at a super market.
- Working for my boss is like driving a car.
- Marriage is like taking a bath.

Mental exercises of this nature represent a tiny investment in time—literally minutes a day—but the results may be startling. Within several weeks you may notice a new expansiveness and breadth in your thinking.

We have found brainstorming to be a particularly useful method for devising new and innovative approaches and solutions to workplace assignments. Before undertaking a new project—or trying to rid yourself of an unwanted feeling or emotion—give your mind free rein and list all the possible ways of approaching and completing the task that you can imagine. Suspend your reason and logic; at this stage do not be concerned with the feasibility of potential approaches and solutions. Value judgments will put blinders on your vision, limit your thinking, and blunt your creativity. Evaluation of the cost effectiveness, practicality, or appropriateness of the ideas you are listing should be made only after you have recorded the widest possible variety of approaches and solutions. Although brainstorming is hardly new, it remains one of the most effective methods for devising alternatives to traditional practices. It is especially productive when done with a group.

Finally, we believe that one of the greatest impediments to creativity in the workplace is the fear of failing. Creativity demands risk taking. New ideas, methods, approaches, and solutions often do not work; miscalculation, foundering, and running aground are risks one takes when sailing into unchartered waters. Yet we hope that the possibility of failing will not deter you. If you wish to try a new tack, an innovative approach to an assignment, a fresh method, or if your job is boring and you wish to try an idea that may energize it, ask your boss for clearance while letting him or her know that your plan might not work. We suspect that he or she will welcome your initiative, inventiveness, and spirit, regardless of the outcome. Remember that the word *play* carries with it the notion of freedom—freedom to try something new, freedom to experiment, and freedom to fail.

A TIME FOR EVERY SEASON

Change, we realize, is never easy, especially when one has let a problem persist. Boredom, for instance, often saps an individual of the will to change; feelings of intimidation may become so habitual that one cannot imagine ever feeling differently; anger may become so ingrained that one forgets what it feels like to react calmly. We hope that *Work Is Not a Four-Letter Word* will help you to make the necessary changes in your working life and will help you develop both the confidence to confront negative feelings and emotions and a methodology for overcoming them. Change, however, also demands courage, and ultimately that must come from within you. We hope that once the needed change occurs, work *will be* a four-letter word: play.

Index

KIN CARE AND THE AMERICAN CORPORATION: Solving the Work/Family Dilemma, by Dayle M. Smith

An inside look at the best kin care plans and programs of more than 100 major companies in all regions of the country. You'll find detailed, real-life accounts of how companies and employees are working together to develop programs that address child and elder care issues. ISBN: 1-55623-449-X $24.95

WORKFORCE AMERICA! Managing Employee Diversity as a Vital Resource, by Marilyn Loden and Judy B. Rosener

A straightforward, practical guide that shows how to manage diversity so it becomes a vital resource that increases creativity, innovation, and enhances productivity. You'll see how to rectify organizational problems that can inhibit the full participation of many diverse employees. ISBN: 1-55623-386-8 $24.95

HOW TO MAKE YOUR BOSS WORK FOR YOU: More Than 200 Hard-Hitting Strategies, Tips, and Tactics to Keep Your Career on the Fast Track, by Jim G. Germer

An innovative, tough, comprehensive, and honest plan for success in today's business environment. Germer gives you a complete game plan for overcoming 10 tough career obstacles in the '90s, strategies to master office politics, and 10 shortcuts to break into middle or upper management. ISBN: 1-55623-417-1 $18.95

SECOND TO NONE: How Our Smartest Companies Put People First, by Charles Garfield

Discover how you can create a workplace where both people and profits flourish! Charles Garfield, best-selling author of *Peak Performers*, gives you an inside look at today's leading businesses and how they became masters at expanding the teamwork and creativity of their workforce. ISBN: 1-55623-360-4 $22.95

THE NO-PAIN RESUME WORKBOOK: A Complete Guide to Job-Winning Resumes, by Hiyaguha Cohen

Cohen makes the enormous task of selling yourself easier. Instead of preaching resume philosophy, you'll find easy-to-use, step-by-step forms with much of the wording already provided. Fill in the blanks and by the time you finish the book, you'll have a unique, powerful resume that will emphasize your assets and creatively conceal your weaknesses. ISBN: 1-55623-577-1 $14.95 (paper)

SELF-DIRECTED WORK-TEAMS: The New American Challenge, by Jack B. Orsburn, Linda Moran, Ed Musselwhite, and John H. Zenger

Show employees from diverse areas of your company how to work together more efficiently and compete more effectively! You'll find how to increase employee productivity, motivate line employees and improve job performance, and reduce the need for layers of corporate bureaucracy. ISBN: 1-55623-341-8 $39.95

Prices quoted are in U.S. currency and are subject to change without notice. Available at Fine Bookstores and Libraries Everywhere.